CHOOSING SCHOOLS AND CHILD CARE OPTIONS
Answering Parents' Questions

ABOUT THE AUTHOR

Nancy H. Phillips teaches in the School of Education and Human Development at Lynchburg College in Lynchburg, Virginia. She holds a doctoral degree in Curriculum and Instruction from the University of Michigan (Ann Arbor) with an emphasis in Emergent Literacy. Doctor Phillips established and directed the Bickham Early Learning Lab School for at-risk four-year-olds at Lynchburg College. This experience helped her gain a working knowledge of state and federal licensing requirements for child day-care centers.

Doctor Phillips was a teacher and an administrator in the public school arena for eighteen years before she switched to higher education. Currently she teaches a variety of early childhood courses to preservice and inservice teachers. She is past president of the local chapter of the National Association for the Education of Young Children (NAEYC) and a board member of the state organization.

Doctor Phillips and her husband live in Lynchburg where they both look forward to visits with their four children and seven grandchildren.

CHOOSING SCHOOLS AND CHILD CARE OPTIONS

Answering Parents' Questions

By

NANCY H. PHILLIPS, ED.D.

CHARLES C THOMAS • PUBLISHER
Springfield • Illinois • U.S.A.

Published and Distributed Throughout the World by
CHARLES C THOMAS • PUBLISHER
2600 South First Street
Springfield, Illinois 62794-9265

This book is protected by copyright. No part of
it may be reproduced in any manner without
written permission from the publisher.

© *1994 by* CHARLES C THOMAS • PUBLISHER
ISBN 0-398-05923-3
Library of Congress Catalog Card Number: 94-19163

With THOMAS BOOKS *careful attention is given to all details of manufacturing and design. It is the Publisher's desire to present books that are satisfactory as to their physical qualities and artistic possibilities and appropriate for their particular use.* THOMAS BOOKS *will be true to those laws of quality that assure a good name and good will.*

Printed in the United States of America
SC-R-3

Library of Congress Cataloging-in-Publication Data
Phillips, Nancy H.
    Choosing schools and child care options : answering parents' questions / by Nancy H. Phillips.
      p.   cm.
    Includes bibliographical references and index.
    ISBN 0-398-05923-3
    1. School choice—United States. 2. Child care services—United States. 3. Education, Preschool—Parent participation—United States. 4. Kindergarten—United States. I. Title.
LB1027.9.P45   1994
372.21—dc20   94-19163
                                                                       CIP

For my grandchildren:
Dawn, Will, Kali, Cortney,
Morgan, Hunter and Meredith

INTRODUCTION

As a parent, you must make decisions for your children which concern their care and nurturing away from your home. Frequently, these decisions are difficult because you have numerous options and not enough information to make choices comfortably. This book is organized to help you make the best choices about child care, preschool and kindergarten placements for your family through reviews of typical questions other parents ask about schooling decisions and with information that equips you to compare preschools. These discussions can help you to decide what is best for your family.

The first chapter is a resource section based on current research and educational theory. It provides you with a brief summary of the best and most recent thought on early childhood issues. This furnishes you with the information that helps you understand how and why schools and child day centers differ. Although the initial chapter is general in nature, each following chapter relates to a specific age group. You can read the introduction and then jump to the age group which concerns you, or you can read the book through chronologically. Each age group chapter discusses typical children in that age group and it answers questions their parents ask. There are options for you to consider and actions you can take when you decide to select specific types of child care or preschools.

Although each chapter repeats some of the information that is relevant to all age groups, each chapter includes pertinent new information for each individual age group. There is an additional chapter that deals specifically with the problems surrounding the child care choices for special needs/handicapped youngsters, and there is information for parents who work part-time and for parents who work unusual schedules.

In addition, the final chapter discusses the legal issues which concern you such as how to report child care wages to social security and other information about the Internal Revenue Service's regulations which deal with child care. The Appendix has information that is generic to all age groups including the resource and referral programs developing in many communities, lists of professional guidelines, and check sheets to use when visiting prospective child care providers. Good luck, and I hope your questions about schools and child care are answered.

N.H.P.

CONTENTS

	Page
Introduction	vii
1. What Should Young Children Be Learning?	3
2. Birth to 18 Months	14
3. 18 Months to Three Years	25
4. Three-Year-Olds	35
5. Four-Year-Olds	46
6. Five-Year-Olds	58
7. Problems for Families Seeking Child Care	69
Children with Special Needs	69
Parents Who Work Unusual Hours	74
Legal and Tax Responsibilities for Child Care	76
Appendices	
A. Child Day Care Check Sheet	81
B. Observations You Make	83
C. Tax Forms	85
D. Licensing and Resource & Referral Services by State Listing	91
Index	99

CHOOSING SCHOOLS
AND
CHILD CARE OPTIONS
Answering Parents' Questions

Chapter 1

WHAT SHOULD YOUNG CHILDREN BE LEARNING?

When you get a group of young parents together in the same room, what generally happens? They talk about their children. Whether they are taking a lunch break, attending a church social, or at a neighborhood park get-together, inevitably conversation revolves around their concerns about their children and their ongoing battles to obtain good child care and to choose the best schools for their family. Imagine you are sitting in a corner of the room and these are some examples of the topics those parents discuss:

Melanie has a fifteen-month-old boy whose sitter plops him in front of the television to keep him amused. She feels concerned about the lack of stimulation he receives and she wants to explore placing him in a child day-care program. She asks the others if they think he is old enough to be placed in a large group situation at a child day center. She worries that other children will overwhelm him.

Brent is a single parent raising a three-year-old girl. The child spends long hours with a sitter who cares for three younger children, and her play appears to be very immature. He wants to know if it is time to enroll her in a preschool where she will be taught her letters and numbers.

Rita's grandmother cares for Rita's little four-year-old girl while Rita works to support herself and the child. Grandma allows the child to do whatever she pleases, and Rita notices the little girl has a difficult time playing with other children. She has not developed ideas about sharing or taking turns. Rita wonders if a play school environment will help her daughter to develop those social skills.

Mary and John's little boy just turned five last week and he is old enough to start kindergarten next month. They voice concern that he is too immature, and they want to know if they should hold him out of school for a year to give him a better chance when he does start school. Will it hurt to keep him at home?

On the other hand, Jan and David's little girl will not be five until December. She passed the tests their public school system gives kindergartners, and they need to decide if it is appropriate to let her begin kindergarten at such a young age.

Benjamin thinks his son's lack of enthusiasm for going to prekindergarten indicates boredom with the program. The children do nothing but play all day, and he thinks his son needs some academic stimulation.

Each of these parents worries about the kinds of child care/schooling decisions that puzzle most parents in today's busy, work-oriented world. This book addresses the issues that make these choices so difficult, and it gives parents, like you, the information to help you make decisions about the kinds of child care you want for your children and which types of schooling are appropriate for children at different ages.

Before considering specific questions, however, you need to review the various philosophies about how children learn, because schools, preschools, and child day centers are established to reflect the specific curriculum philosophies of their planners. You need to decide which type of school setting is the most appropriate for your child before you can begin selecting schools or investigating child care options.

WHAT DO THE EXPERTS SAY?

There are three major approaches to early childhood education, and educators label these the *romanticist,* the *behaviorist,* and the *constructivist* approaches to educating young children. There are some metaphors used by early childhood experts that may help you understand how they describe children's learning. The romanticist considers the young child to be like a new flower unfolding, or a plant growing. You can see this influence when you look at the word "kindergarten," because the father of that concept, Friedrich Froebel, coined that term using the two German words, *kinder* (child) and *garten* (garden). The romanticist's school is child-centered, which means the children (not the teachers) determine what goes on in the classroom. Followers of this approach believe that if you place children in an environment properly arranged with learning opportunities and with teachers who watch as the children do what they choose to do, the children will learn (grow).

The second theoretical approach to early learning is the behaviorist approach, and the metaphor for this approach compares the child to a machine. The school determines what the child must learn, and teachers design activities to assure that this material is learned—something like putting gas into a motor (the machine) to make it run. Another metaphor for the behaviorist's learner is the little computer that teachers program. The behaviorist school is teacher-centered with the teacher responsible for choosing what the child learns. Children have little or no choices in their daily activities at these schools, and they spend much of their time in large group activities or in completing work sheets at tables.

The third approach to educating young children is the constructivist approach which is more difficult to represent with a metaphor. Experts use the term "child philosopher" to describe this learner because they encourage the child to discover new information and to ask questions about what he unearths. They believe children cannot be given knowledge from without; they have to construct it within themselves. The child and the teacher share responsibility for initiating learning, with the teacher providing the scaffolding for the child's climb to greater understanding. Here is an example which shows you how to differentiate among these approaches.

Pretend you are watching preschool children who will learn that if they mix and combine colors they will create new colors. Today's lesson is about blue and yellow colors and the children will learn to create the new color, *green.* In the romanticist school the children use paints every day, and when curious children accidentally mix the two colors of blue and yellow, they discover they create *green.* Some children in the class never take the time to go to the art center to experiment with those colors. They do not learn about *green.* Other children experiment with mixing all of the colors, and some create *green* while others discover nothing more interesting than huge brownish/black splotches.

If the children attend a school patterned after the behaviorist theory, the teacher gives the class a lecture on mixing paints, she tells them how to mix blue and yellow, she directs them in which proportions to use, and then she gives them a work sheet to practice this new information. Twenty-five beautiful pictures of yellow flowers with green leaves planted in blue pots will hang in the hall outside their classroom. This is direct instruction of information that the school decides the students need to learn.

In the constructivist classroom, the teacher sets up a different art center daily. One day the teacher has blue and yellow paints, brushes, and large sheets of unruled paper in the center. The teacher suggests that the children may want to mix the paints, but she does not tell them which proportions to use. The children discover different hues of blue green and yellow green as they create designs of their own. They experiment with two parts blue and one part yellow and they observe how that color differs from one made of two parts yellow and one part blue. On another day there is a cookie sheet with globs of yellow and blue fingerpaint sitting out on the table to tempt the curious child who wants to smear the colored paint around and discover a glorious blue/yellow/green colored picture that the teacher can save by making a print of it on paper. The teacher guides and gives answers to questions and observations, but she does not tell the children how to use the colors in the center. She encourages all to take a turn in the color center, but no child must participate.

These are very simplified examples of how teachers use the three different theoretical approaches to teaching young children in the classroom. Either the classes are child-centered, teacher-centered, or the children and the teacher cooperate in learning. If you want more detailed information on these three approaches, there is a list of recommended books at the end of the chapter.

In addition to these three major approaches to classroom organization, there are three other beliefs that control the major everyday curriculum decisions teachers make within the classroom. These three are: (1) the use of developmentally appropriate activities for children; (2) the academic activity guidelines for encouraging children's emerging literacy; and (3) the importance of play in a child's day. As you look at schools and child day centers, investigate or observe each school's approach to learning by comparing how they address these three issues. The school you choose should provide the learning atmosphere where you decide your child learns best. A closer examination of these three concepts reveals the type of activities you need to compare.

DEVELOPMENTALLY APPROPRIATE PRACTICES

The first issue for you to examine developed from the growing consensus that all children should be placed in learning environments that are developmentally appropriate for them. The National Association for the Education of Young Children (Bredekamp, 1986) publishes guidelines for developmentally appropriate practices and environments for children, and most educational publications and interest groups endorse these guidelines for anyone working with young children ages birth to eight years. These guidelines state that children should not be required to do those activities which are not developmentally appropriate for them. This appropriateness is not just age appropriateness, it is individual child appropriateness. What is appropriate for a child who has well-developed fine motor skills is not appropriate for one who does not.

For example, some preschools require four-year-olds to learn to write their alphabet letters on lined paper. This is generally an inappropriate activity for four-year-olds, because (1) most of them are still gaining control of the fine motor skills required for writing, and (2) many of them have not developed an interest in print and they do not have an understanding of what the letters represent. If they do not understand why they are writing those letters, then the exercise becomes meaningless. If teachers chastise them for drawing the letters incorrectly—upside down or backwards—they are criticizing the children for their slower rates of fine motor development. There are exceptions, of course, and some children do have a strong interest in their letters and want to write them when they are four years old. This type of activity is appropriate only for those children with both a demonstrated interest in print and fine motor agility. If you visit a preschool that requires all four-year-olds to sit down at tables and do work sheets on the letters of the alphabet, ask yourself or one of the staff whether this preschool is aware of the current emphasis on developmentally appropriate practices. Many preschool owners and teachers do not have an early childhood educational background. Question whether your own four-year-old is ready or eager to spend the day doing this type of activity.

Whole group activities are not developmentally appropriate for most young children. These types of activities should be limited to brief morning circle discussions about topics like the weather and for those times during the day when the teacher reads aloud to the class. It is more appropriate for these children to have activity choices and for them to have the freedom to roam from choice to choice. Most of them have not developed the attention span necessary to sit for long periods of time, and they enjoy the movement, problem solving, and socializing opportunities learning centers provide. Children run the risk of being misdiagnosed as hyperactive in preschool if they are required to do developmentally inappropriate activities that require them to sit for long periods of time.

A child does not develop an attention span by being *made* to sit still, and one quick way to assure a youngster will dislike school is to demand too much sitting-still time from him/her. The wiggle worm needs to be up and about developing those fine and gross motor skills that are important for that child now. Children develop motor skills at different ages just as all children walk at different ages, talk at different ages, and sleep all night at different ages. This is the reason why teachers must allow children to do those activities that are developmentally appropriate for them individually.

EMERGING LITERACY

The second issue revolves around a concept educators formerly called *school readiness.* We know now that children do not wake up on their fifth birthday ready to learn to read and write. Their knowledge of print and the written word develops slowly just as their language and their motor skills become better defined as they grow. All children do not walk at nine months of age, and neither are all five-year-olds ready to learn to read. The process of gradually becoming prepared to learn to read and write is currently referred to as a child's *emerging literacy.*

Parents and teachers provide input for the child's emerging sense of what books and reading are all about. They read to children to entertain them, but in the process the children learn that books have a front and back, the print starts at the top of the page and it goes from left to right on the page, books have a special language (like "Once upon a time..." and "They all lived happily ever after"), and letters represent sounds that make words. The more books they see and hear, the better and earlier these lessons are learned.

The process is not complete, however, unless children have opportunities to practice what they learn on paper. It is important that each child has the opportunity to develop from a scribbler to a child who starts imitating print around her (like the big M over McDonald's), and then starts trying to write her own words. The child is not ready to read until she associates print with words, and actually begins putting sounds to letters that she writes as she invents spellings for stories she wants to tell, shopping lists she makes, or pictures she labels.

Teachers can force children to form letters, but they cannot force the background knowledge that reading and writing skills need in order to develop. Requiring a child to write letters and memorize the alphabet song will be meaningless if that child has not gained a sense of how and why print represents words. This knowledge comes gradually, and a good preschool will include a great amount of reading aloud to young children in its program as well as opportunities for them to do unstructured writing. Search out a school for your children that encourages their emerging literacy rather than one that claims to teach them the alphabet. There is a popular poster that lists the ten ways to become a good reader: READ, READ, READ, READ, READ, READ, READ, READ, READ, and READ. Change that poster to say the ten ways to teach young children to read are READ TO THEM, READ TO THEM, READ TO THEM, READ TO THEM, READ TO THEM, READ TO THEM, READ TO THEM, READ TO THEM, READ TO THEM, and READ TO THEM!

PLAY

One of the most abused notions in education is that of the value of children's play. How often have you heard someone ask, "How can you fail kindergarten? All they do is play." Before public kindergartens became part of most public school programs, children's kindergarten days were filled with painting, sandpile art, block building, and musical games. Even though educators knew that a great deal of learning occurred during children's play, in the past decade there was a demand for kindergartners to learn to read, write, and spell. However, the United States fell behind the rest of the world academically during that emphasis on academic preschools and kindergartens. As schools pushed these academic activities down from their first grade classes to their newly created public school kindergartens, more and more children began to have problems in school and to be retained.

Our national illiteracy rate reached an all-time high this year. Some estimates suggest one of every four adults is illiterate, while a recent report of the National Assessment of Educational Progress study (September, 1993) claims half of our adults are illiterate. Recent research (Shepard & Smith, 1987) shows the emphasis on academic activities for very young children helped to create the large group of unsuccessful learners in our country. Since teaching four- and five-year-olds to read has not worked, early childhood specialists urge schools and preschools to return to more developmentally appropriate practices in the early years with play as an integral part of programs for young children.

Montessori said that play was a child's work, but what did she mean by *play*? Why is play important? Play involves much more than children interacting with toys. Rogers and Sawyers (1988) say play is the only human behavior that integrates and balances all aspects of human functioning. No one tells children how to play or what to do—they explore their environment or a new toy naturally and then they decide how to use it in their play. That activity ceases to be play if adults structure or even interfere inappropriately with that play. When a child is told "how" to play with things, he does not have the opportunity to investigate, to experiment, to be creative, or to experience success in his own way. Children who are self-motivated enjoy the activity for itself.

Caldwell (1985) says play is something you do not have to do well, it is just fun. Unlike adults, children will try a variety of activities and they will not be disappointed when they do not excel. They do not understand "rules" and their play should not involve games with rules until they are seven or eight years old. Play changes as children mature. Children ages two to seven engage in symbolic play where they pretend to talk on the phone, feed their baby dolls, pour pretend glasses of milk, board pretend school buses, and practice being mommies and daddies.

Parten (1932) defined the different types of children's play in terms of the categories of social play with their peers. *Unoccupied* children watch others play, but they do not join in. Some children are *onlookers* who watch others play, ask questions about that activity and perhaps move in closer to get a better view. A child who plays alone with objects is a *solitary independent* player who is not interacting with others. *Parallel activity* involves children playing beside other children but not with them—perhaps in a sandbox. *Associative* play has children exchanging toys, but no organized projects are under way such as building a fort. When children agree to undertake a project like a fort, they engage in *cooperative* play and one or more of the children take over as leaders. Children need to experience all of these types of play in their developmental process because this is how they learn their social skills—sharing, bartering, compromising, and problem solving. A preschool that does not allow children a great amount of time to play freely does not promote that social development.

When you visit a preschool or child day center, look for the types of play activities that are developmentally appropriate for young children. Classrooms that are well-planned for young children will have a number of "centers" to encourage constructive play activities. One of the most important of these is the dramatic play center. Often schools have this area set up as a housekeeping center where children practice being parents, taking care of children, and fixing meals. Other dramatic centers create fire stations, grocery stores, doctor's offices, and automotive service centers. Each of these centers allows children to pretend to be what they will be in the grownup world. These centers must be readily accessible to both girls and boys because boys need to play with dolls in order to grow up to be good daddies, and girls need to know that they, too, are future firemen, doctors, and race car drivers. Frown on any school situations that have "girl" and "boy" areas, because they retain the old stereotypical ideas of male and female roles.

Another important play area to look for is the block center. This is one of the most important centers for all children, for here they construct and problem solve just as they will in the real world. Children building bridges together use language skills, solve building glitches, and create works of art. The blocks should be made of different materials (wood, cardboard, foam) and should be different sizes and weights. The block center can be located near the housekeeping center to encourage children to build more rooms on the house, or near the small manipulatives center where cars, trucks, and zoo animals are available for inclusion in some grand designs. Knowledgeable teachers take instant photos of large building projects so that parents and friends can admire them long after the blocks are returned to the shelves at cleanup time.

The art/writing center offers a variety of activities. There should be paper, pencils, crayons, and markers ready for children to use at all times. While special projects for holidays are interesting and parents expect teachers to come up with cute ideas for their refrigerator galleries, beware of the classroom where each child has the same picture (such as a turkey) and is told exactly how to color it. There is nothing creative going on in that atmosphere. Also, if art activities require adult hands to do things like staple, cut, and glue, those activities are not age-appropriate for the children involved, and only uninformed parents will be happy with the results. Why not have a purple turkey with his tail on top of his back? A child sees things her own way, and she is encouraged to express her creative ideas in a center that has different and interesting materials at her beck and call.

Another important feature of that art/writing center is the support it provides children in their emerging knowledge about writing. Children need opportunities to experience the stages of writing—drawing, scribbling, copying environmental print and letter strings, making letter/sound connections, and invented spellings—before they are ready for reading instruction. When teachers give children opportunities to write (prescriptions in the doctor's office, grocery lists in the housekeeping center) and to tell stories on paper, they support the emerging literacy process. These materials can be a part of the art center, or the teacher may set up a separate writing center.

A woodworking center gives the children opportunities to saw, hammer, and to build. They get involved in designing, planning, constructing, problem solving and completing their own ideas. The sensory center has a water table (sometimes filled with other materials such as cornstarch, sand, or small gravel) that allows children to experiment with weights and measurements and encourages them to experience how differently things can feel. Music centers encourage rhythmic activities, reading centers allow children to browse around the world of books, and science centers help to develop their knowledge about how plants grow, how rain evaporates, and how sugar and salt differ. Children are learning when they are involved in these kinds of center activities. They do not have to sit still and be quiet for long periods of time, and they can choose those activities which interest them. Beware of group sessions where all the children are doing the same activity at the same time. These are not effective learning experiences.

Other play features to look for in a prospective preschool or kindergarten include indoor and outdoor equipment that both encourages large muscle development, and allows the children to create uses for that equipment. A large round concrete tube can be an imaginative child's bear cave, a car tunnel, or a bedroom. A beautifully outfitted wooden train engine will be played with only as a train engine. For safety's sake, the outside equipment should have pits of soft mulch or sand in the areas where children are likely to fall—at the end of the sliding board, for example.

You have an idea, now, about the classrooms and learning environments you may discover when you are choosing a school for your children. As you begin visiting preschools and child day centers, keep your eyes open for these different program features. You want a school that understands developmentally appropriate practices, a school whose teachers read frequently to the children and give them opportunities to develop their emerging writing skills, and a school that knows play is an important physical, social and problem-solving activity for all children.

The following chapters will help you consider the specific problems and schooling options for children who fall into five different age groups:

birth to 18 months (Chap. 2); eighteen months to three years (Chap. 3); three-year-olds (Chap. 4); four-year-olds (Chap. 5); and five-year-olds (Chap. 6). The last chapter discusses special needs/handicapped youngsters, parents with unusual schedules, and then the legal and tax issues that concern parents seeking child care (Chap. 7). Feel free to skip to the chapter that discusses your child's age group.

REFERENCES

Bredekamp, S. (Ed.) (1986). *Developmentally appropriate practice.* Washington, D.C.: National Association for the Education of Young Children.

Caldwell, B. M. (1985). Parent-child play: A playful evaluation. In C. C. Brown & A. W. Gottfried (Eds.), *Play interactions: The role of toys and parental involvement in children's development* (pp. 167–178). Skillman, NJ: Johnson & Johnson.

DeVries, R., & Kohlberg, L. (1990). *Constructivist early education: Overview and comparison with other programs.* Washington, D.C.: National Association for the Education of Young Children.

Frost, J. L. (1992). *Play and playscapes.* New York: Delmar.

Henry, Tamara. (September 16, 1993). TV gets blame for poor reading. *USA TODAY,* p. D1.

Parten, M. B. (1932). Social participation among preschool children. *Journal of Abnormal Psychology, 27,* 243–269.

Rogers, C. S., & Sawyers, J. K. (1988). *Play in the lives of children.* Washington, D.C.: National Association for the Education of Young Children.

Shepard, L. S., & Smith, M. L. (1987). Flunking kindergarten: Escalating curriculum leaves many behind. *American Educator, 12*(2), 34–38.

Chapter 2

BIRTH TO 18 MONTHS

Most of you who are looking for infant child care are parents who work outside of your home on a regularly scheduled basis. Pregnant mothers begin the arduous task of finding sitters for their children-to-be months before they stop work and take maternity leave. Some women are lucky enough to have mothers, grandmothers, or sisters who volunteer to take care of the new baby. Most of you are not so lucky. Some of you are torn with guilt over leaving your babies at all, while others are eager to get back to jobs that they enjoy immensely although they are fearful of letting someone else raise their infants. Many of you have no choice but to seek some type of care for your young babies because you work out of necessity.

This chapter attempts to answer the questions of parents who seek infant care. The questions are general in nature, and the answers should help parents with similar questions.

What type of child care do you recommend for babies?

When you select your child care provider you need to be concerned about the three major needs of your baby: a need for cuddling and security, the need for a healthy and safe environment, and the need for someone who will promote his language development process.

If you decide to investigate the different child care options listed later in this chapter, search for those that offer the best opportunity for finding a caregiver who will meet your baby's first need for cuddling and security. They can do this by holding and rocking him as he takes his bottle rather than propping it on a pillow for him—babies thrive on this kind of closeness. Babies also need to know that if they cry, someone listens and pays attention to their needs. Insecurity develops in babies when no one answers their pleas for a dry diaper, a bottle, or a discarded toy.

Your baby's health and safety are extremely important to you, and you need a provider who meets this second major need for a secure environment. Will your sitter change the baby's diapers frequently to prevent uncomfortable rashes? If your baby shares a sitter with other children, does the sitter/center provide a place for him to sleep on clean sheets, drink from his own cup or bottle, and does the sitter use record-keeping procedures that guarantee your baby takes his own medicine? A licensed center undergoes inspections for areas where lead paint can poison children, scalding water faucets can burn them, and uncovered electric plugs can lead to electrical shocks. Do the sitters you are considering maintain the same types of secure environments?

Finally, you need to know that your child's language development— his third need—continues on schedule. He needs to have the same stimulating language experiences with a sitter that he has when he is with you. Be aware that your baby can pick up the language patterns of his sitter, and poor English or a heavy foreign accent may confuse or delay his language development. This is the period in a baby's life when adults model language by labeling everything in the child's environment— CAR, BABY, MOMMY, COOKIE. As the baby's vocabulary increases, he begins to put words together in telegraphic phrases like ME GO and DADDY BYE-BYE. At this point in the language process the baby needs adults who expand his language. If a baby says, "ME GO," the adult needs to answer, "Yes, honey. You are going to go with me." For "DADDY BYE-BYE" the adult expands by saying, "Daddy has gone bye-bye to work." This is how adults model good language patterns. You want your baby's language to grow even when you are not around him.

This is a time, too, when adults should show the baby about his world. "See that cow? The cow says, "MOO!" or "Don't touch that! It is hot, and it will hurt you." It is a time to begin reading repetitive stories to your baby. Examples of these are the old favorites such as *The Gingerbread Boy* ("I got away from the little old man, and the little old woman..."), *The Little Red Hen* ("Not I!" said the duck. "Not I!" said the pig), and Bill Martin's *Brown Bear* ("Brown Bear, Brown Bear, What do you see? I see a...."). This is the perfect time, also, to begin reading Mother Goose's old favorite nursery rhymes to babies because they introduce the wonderful sounds of our language.

Each of these activities—showing, talking about, and reading—spurs the young child's language development. When you look at a child care placement for your baby, language development should be a very important factor for you. Books are better language models than TV soap operas, and you want a care provider who knows how important it is to read to very young children several times each day rather than propping them up in front of the television. When someone holds your baby on her lap and reads to him, she is providing all of his needs—a feeling of security, a safe environment, and the language development he needs.

My baby screams bloody murder because he knows I am about to leave him with the sitter. Should I change my child care arrangements?

All babies go through stages of clinging to a parent and acting like they will die if mom leaves them behind. If the sitter/child care provider is someone you trust and someone your baby knows well, make your leave taking short and sweet and get out of sight. In no time at all your baby will be happy and clinging to the sitter. You are not abusing this child, and if you are sure that the sitter is taking good care of your infant, then go on to work without any guilt.

You need to be concerned with a first-time sitter. Have her visit with the baby a day before you are actually going to leave him in her care, or go visit a center and stay with your baby as he becomes acquainted with the staff. Strangers are scary for children in this age group, and you want to ease their separation anxiety.

Next, you should establish a routine that allows you to deliver your baby to the sitter unhurriedly, a smile on your face and in your voice so that the baby feels safe, secure and loved. Just pitching a baby into the hands of a waiting caretaker and rushing off is reason enough to make any baby unhappy and insecure. Before you go to bed at night, pack the baby's diaper bag with the necessary equipment for the following day, making sure a treasured, familiar toy is included. Some emergency is bound to arise if you wait until morning to do this chore, and then you are more apt to arrive at the sitter's in a rush and you leave a squealing baby behind.

Why can't I find a center that will take both my infant and my four-year-old?

Child day centers must meet a large number of regulations when they seek licensing. Infant care regulations are different from those pertaining to older children, and many child day centers choose not to apply for an infant license. For instance, infants require that elaborate diaper-changing regulations be met: the children cannot be diapered in the same room they play, workers must don gloves, hot water must be available at the changing site, and proper disposal of used diapers is monitored. Infants require a much smaller child-to-care provider ratio, so a center has to hire more employees if they accept infants. The cribs, playpens and other baby equipment take up more of the center's square footage. Those areas have to be quiet for naptime, and many centers just do not have adequate space for keeping all age groups. Although this is inconvenient for the parent with both an infant and an older preschooler, joint placements in centers will continue to be hard to find.

Why won't my child day center let my son bring his teddy bear with him?

This situation occurs at a center where the rules and regulations are established by someone who does not have a strong early childhood educational background. For instance, there was one center that was run by two former elementary school teachers who were great teachers of older children but whose educational background did not include early childhood courses. They kept the children from fighting over toys by telling the parents that they were not allowed to bring toys to the center. You can keep third graders from bringing teddy bears to school, but infants who are attached to a particular item such as a teddy bear or a blanket need to be able to take that security item with them each day. Some centers have a special place (such as the child's crib) where the item must be kept so no other child will grab it. Old teddy bears can be disease carriers, they can cause fights over possession rights, and they can look very shabby. They can also provide the security many children need when their parents have left them for the day.

If your center tells you that you cannot bring that teddy, ask them why. Tell them you understand that good early childhood practice recognizes the importance of that teddy, and that you hope they will make an adjustment in their policy. If they do not, look for another placement.

What are the options available for infant child care?

No one type of child care is just right for all families. You need to approach that decision only after discovering what is available in your community and after comparing the costs in time and money for you and your family. There are multiple options for mothers of children in this age group. People who live in large urban areas have more choices than those who live in small towns. However, the costs of some types of child care make them out of reach for most parents, and other parents do not have transportation to take babies to more desirable centers.

The discussion for each option describes that option's advantages and disadvantages. This helps you to weigh whether it is a viable option for you. You must be aware of the pitfalls found with some types of child care, and you must be on guard against those problems. Every parent has the right to observe a child care placement at length before deciding to leave a child with a provider. You also have the right (and the responsibility) to make unannounced visits to the facility to check on your child and the type of care he receives. If a center or sitter refuses to allow you to visit unannounced, you should immediately wonder what it is they are afraid you will see or hear. Other parents are wonderful resources for recommending child care providers, but do not accept their recommendations without investigating that placement just as thoroughly as you would any other. Here are the options your community may offer:

1. *A relative keeps the child.* Parents consider this the ideal arrangement — mother, sister, brother, aunt or grandma keeps the baby. This is usually the least expensive form of child care available, especially if the relative is willing to do it with little or no charge to you. Most relatives are willing to keep pediatrician appointments or take a sick baby to the doctor for the parents. However, there are some definite drawbacks to having a relative keep your baby. Specific things to note when you choose this kind of provider:

- a. You must have a backup available on a moment's notice in case the primary sitter gets sick or breaks a leg, wants to go shopping, or goes on a vacation.
- b. Unless you keep very careful records of payment by check, you are unable to claim your income tax deduction for child care when you pay a relative. You must pay the employer's portion of social security deductions for them and pay unemployment taxes.
- c. It is harder to criticize a relative if you disapprove of some practice the relative has concerning your baby. What a way to start a family argument!
- d. If the relative is older (like a grandparent), make sure she still possesses the unending patience babies require. You know how distressed you get when your baby will not take a nap. Can that older person hang in there and keep a sunny disposition during teething bouts and other periods of distress?

2. *Get a nanny.* Two young lawyers in the Washington, D.C. area advertised for a college-educated nanny for their children and offered an $18,000 starting salary. There was also a recent story in *The New York Times* (April 14, 1993) about how people pay nannies poorly (national

average is $200 to $250 a week) and take advantage of uneducated young women who have no training for other jobs. Those women were paid minimum wage and they worked twelve hours a day, seven days a week.

If you decide to get a nanny, do a good job of investigating your rights as well as your responsibilities. According to the *Times* article, federal law requires nannies be paid minimum wage (currently $4.25) and allows employers to deduct a small fee for room and board which in New York equals $6.15 per day. You must pay social security and unemployment taxes in addition.

There are schools and agencies which claim they train nannies with the proper child rearing information to provide parents with a peace of mind while they are at work. Check out the reliability of these schools, and find out what services they provide in meeting payroll taxes. Remember, a nanny is not on duty 24 hours a day. She needs regular hours, days off, a private room, and she needs to fit into the intimate life of your family.

In actuality, many nannies are foreign-born young women called "au pairs" who are looking for an adventure living abroad or for an opportunity to attend night classes in this country while working. They trade off sitting with your children for their room and board since it is difficult for them to get the "green card" they need if they work in the United States.

Nannies generally have full responsibility for the children in their care but are not necessarily housekeepers. They live in the home and receive room and board as the major part of their salaries. Au pairs offer an international flavor to child care and may introduce your child to another language. Specific things to note when you choose this kind of provider:

   a. Contracts are usually for one year. Some people find they are changing nannies frequently.
   b. Unless you go through an agency that does the criminal checks and investigates references, you may be buying an unknown quality of service.
   c. You must file the forms with the IRS and pay the employer's share in order to take your child care tax break. Make sure your nanny has a green card if she is not a U.S. citizen.
   d. You need an instant backup for those days your nanny is off or ill.

3. *Get a sitter to come to your home each day.* This is a comforting option because it means the infant stays in familiar surroundings, sleeps in his

own crib, and knows little change in his daily routine. Sitters who come in for the day may also perform light housekeeping chores and even fix dinner for the family. These sitters charge more than those who keep babies in their own homes. Specific things to note when you choose this kind of provider:

    a. In-home sitters are hard to find, and they are expensive because they want to be paid more than minimum wage if housekeeping chores are added to their job description.

    b. You must pay social security, unemployment taxes, and income withholding taxes.

    c. You need a backup for days when the sitter is sick or unavailable.

    d. You can require the sitter to have a criminal check through the state police so that you will know she has no record of abusive behavior.

  4. *Take your child to the home of someone who takes care of several children in her home.* This category of sitter needs to be divided into two subcategories. One group of family day-care workers is unlicensed, unregulated and therefore generally cheaper than the other group. These two groups are discussed separately.

In the Baby-sitter's Home — the Unlicensed Sitter

There are ads in newspapers soliciting parents to keep children at the sitter's home. Most of these are reputable baby-sitters. Depending upon the state in which you live, these sitters may not be subject to regulations pertaining to fire safety, personal health standards, criminal checks, or required reference checks. You must ascertain this information yourself. Ask a prospective sitter if you can visit in her home for a morning to see how the day goes for the children in her care. Be aware that one person cannot care for a number of small babies with any degree of quality care, and this is why licensed homes must not exceed a maximum number of infants per adult caretaker.[1] Check whether there is any type of record keeping for how often diapers are changed and medicine is given, or times when the child is fed. Must you bring your own portacrib? If not, will your child share a bed with other children? Does the sitter use rubber gloves when she changes your baby's diaper, and does she dispose

---

1. For instance, effective November, 1993, Virginia limits adult to child ratios for infants to one adult for every four children.

of those gloves before she changes another baby? Does she have an emergency backup sitter in case of her own illness, or will that be your responsibility? Specific things to note when you choose this kind of provider:

    a. These sitters are usually reasonably priced and may request that you pay them in cash so that they do not have to report their income. You are forfeiting your IRS child care deduction if you agree to go along with this payment plan and you are breaking the law.

    b. Be cautious when selecting this type of sitter because there are no controls whatsoever to insure your child against physical or sexual abuse. Generally, regulatory agencies have no jurisdiction in these homes.

    c. Many of these sitters are well-educated mothers (often former teachers) who are choosing to sit for other children in order to stay home with their own children. These can be excellent placements if carefully researched and if you make visits into the home prior to selecting them. Ask them how they will feed your baby, and notice their disciplinary actions. Back off from sitters who yell and scream at their own children, for they will scream at yours.

Licensed Family Day-Care Homes

There are several ways homes earn inclusion in this category. They may be homes that voluntarily register with state regulatory agencies or with resource and referral agencies that provide oversight. They may be homes that joined a family day-care system. The family day-care systems regulate/supervise the homes, provide bookkeeping services to permit patrons IRS deductions and to allow the sitters to meet filing requirements, and they help the sitters by referring clients to them. Specific things to note when you choose this kind of provider:

    a. Family day-care systems often maintain backup homes for substitute sitting when the primary sitter is ill.

    b. The system trains the sitters in child care procedures, health regulations, nutrition guidelines for lunches and snacks, and inservices them in different human growth and development issues that prepare them better for the job they undertake.

c. The system gives their providers training in disciplinary tactics, play options, arts and crafts activities, and first aid.
d. The systems charge fixed rates, bill you regularly, and provide documentation for your IRS child care deduction. You can voice complaints to them and expect a response from them.
e. Providers who voluntarily license their homes demonstrate their knowledge of the importance of providing a proper environment for young children. They make sure they meet fire regulations. They are not going to keep more children than they can provide for safely.

5. *Child day centers.* The final option open to parents of children in the birth to eighteen months old category is the child day center. Licensing is very strict for these types of centers in most states, although some states still do not require church-operated centers to meet licensing regulations. You must seek out those centers that accept infants. Since the staff to child ratio is much lower for infant care, this type of care is the most expensive. When you confirm that the center you are visiting is licensed, then you know a great deal about the physical environment your child will experience. Licensing requires providers to pass environmental tests such as holding asbestos-free certificates, making lead tests of the paint in the rooms, tests of the purity of the water, and even tests of the soil on the playground. Fire protection equipment, alarms, exits, and training are required. Even the water temperature at sinks is checked to be certain children cannot be scalded accidently.

What licensing does not tell you is the kind of emotional atmosphere your child will experience. Is there a rocking chair where an assistant can rock your baby as she gives him a bottle, or are the bottles propped next to the baby in the crib? Will a familiar caretaker have regular care for your infant, or does the center have a policy that the caretaker is changed every two weeks so the children will not become too attached to one person? Specific things to note when you choose this kind of provider:

a. Remember that any business person can open a child day center, and the owner's knowledge of information about children's growth and development is not a requirement for licensing. Make sure your baby is not just a figure on someone's profit and loss sheet.
b. Find out how bottles are marked and stored—is there a chance for a mix-up? Are drinking cups disposable, or at least marked with children's names so that they are not shared?

c. Do the diaper-changing records show frequent diapering?
d. Is there a separate area for sick babies, or must you keep your baby at home every time he has a runny nose?

6. *Employer-sponsored child day centers.* This is an exciting new trend in child care. Basically, a company or corporation realizes that absenteeism is greatest among young parents, and that an effective way to reduce that rate is to participate in providing quality child care for its employees. Some companies set up their own licensed centers on their premises. They are like most licensed centers with the one important exception that the location allows parents to visit their children during the day, and nursing mothers can continue to nurse their babies after returning to work. These centers are usually subsidized by the company and this allows very affordable child care.

Another way companies can participate is to buy slots in regular child day centers and reserve those slots for their employees. Frequently the company subsidizes these slots to lower the employees' child care costs. One other company benefit that companies provide is a payroll deduction of pretax dollars which the employee can use to pay child care costs. This substantially reduces child care costs for the employee. Contact your employer to see if any of these benefits are available to you.

The very best child care provider for your baby is you if you are financially and emotionally able to stay at home with your baby. That is not a viable option for all of you, and the next best approach to child care for infants is to find a care provider who can best substitute for you while you are at work. Parents need the stimulation of their jobs, their contacts with other adults, and the resources working provides. The quality of care you demand during the day must be matched with some quality time for you and your baby when you are home. It is very difficult to have a full-time job, grocery shop, prepare meals, do the laundry, and keep your household running smoothly. Yet each of those things can go undone occasionally to allow you time to sit and play with your baby. Remember to plan some quality time with that special little person every day. Rock your baby, read to him, talk with him, and show him how very much he means to you. Far too soon he will grow up and leave you with a great deal of time to do those things you did not get done when you were sitting in that rocking chair.

Finally, whatever type of child care you decide to select for your infant, consult the center checklists in Appendix A and B for specific things to note when you make a visit and review the questions that you can ask of any prospective caregiver. Do not feel embarrassed about asking providers questions such as, "Do you keep records of how often you diaper the children?" Reasonable child care is very difficult to find, but parents must not be afraid of angering a prospective baby-sitter by asking questions.

Your child's health and welfare is a very serious business, and if you do not determine ahead of time that a provider has no criminal record, it will be too late after you find your child was abused. Remember, if a provider will not allow you to visit, ask questions, and observe his/her program, scratch that provider off your list. There must be something in that program that the provider does not want you to observe.

SPECIAL NOTES AS YOU BEGIN YOUR SEARCH

1. When you begin visiting sitters or centers, go unannounced.
2. If you are not welcomed, drop that name from your list.
3. Check for cleanliness, licensing, posted menus, and signs of record keeping for diapering frequency.
4. Ask if you must provide a portacrib or crib for your baby.
5. Do not be pressured into signing up on the same day you visit with such statements from a center as, "We have one opening, but I won't be able to hold it for you if you do not sign up now."
6. Licensed centers are required to have a parent's policy manual. Ask for a copy and take it home to study. This way you can find out their regulations regarding emergencies and sick babies.

BOOKS FOR FURTHER READING

Elkind, David. (1988). *The hurried child: Growing up too fast too soon.* New York: Addison-Wesley.
Elkind, David. (1987). *Miseducation: Preschoolers at risk.* New York: Knopf.
Katzev, Aphra R., & Bragdon, Nancy H. (1990). *Child care solutions: A parents' guide to finding child care you can trust.* New York: Avon.
Lusk, Diane, & McPherson, Bruce. (1992). *Nothing but the best: Making day care work for you and your child.* New York: Quill.

Chapter 3

EIGHTEEN MONTHS TO THREE YEARS

Toddlers are very busy little people who are learning to run, hop, skip, and jump their way through life. Most children change from babies to independent little people during this time in their lives. They learn to run with alacrity, to jabber endlessly, and they assert themselves by insisting on doing things "byself!" They regularly use about 50 words at eighteen months, and speak in two- or three-word sentences by the time they turn two. Their vocabularies can grow to include as many as 300 words during these years if the adults around them encourage their language.

Toddlers like to be noticed and enjoy having an audience, but they play alone happily. They repeat much of the adult language around them, but they point or say, "uh-uh" still to communicate their needs. Typically they back into chairs to sit down, they love to pull/push objects, they begin to scribble if allowed to have a crayon, and they can point to objects in a picture book if adults spend time reading to them. These children are in the magic years of potty training, and many parents consider changing their child care arrangements about the time their children become toilet trained. Since many centers will not take children until they have taken this momentous step toward independence, it is a natural time for child care choices to change.

This is a time, too, when parents show concern about whether their child is learning the social skills gleaned from playing with other children, and they also wonder whether their sitter is providing enough stimulation to spur the child's language development and creativity. These issues vary in importance from child to child and from family to family.

My little girl is the only child my sitter keeps.
Does she need to be playing with other children at this age?

The answer to this question differs in each family. The youngest child in a family with four siblings gets all of the stimulation she needs when the family is all together in the evenings and on weekends. She may actually thrive on the one-to-one situation a sitter provides. The child with no siblings, cousins, or neighbors will need to have the opportunity to play with other children at some point. A different sitter who keeps other children might be the answer, or a child day center can provide playmates.

Our sitter keeps our two-year-old in the playpen during part of the day. Is this bad for him?

It really depends on how this child spends the rest of his day. At this age children are accomplished walkers and veterans at investigating everything about them. They are guilty of trying to do things to keep up with older children that they cannot quite handle, and this may explain why the sitter uses the playpen. If she keeps him in a playpen just part of the day and gives him manipulative toys and books that interest him, he may do just fine. Children should have opportunities to run and play at this age, but less stimulating activities are good for them, too. Find out how much of the day she keeps him in the playpen, and then decide whether to be concerned.

I have trouble keeping up with my toddler. How can I expect a teacher with eight or ten toddlers in her care to keep up with him?

A safe environment is a major concern for parents of toddlers. For instance, David is your typical toddler, and he fell and cracked his head open five of six straight Sunday mornings while trying to catch up with his older brother right in his own home. His little legs could not match up with his bright ideas for keeping himself occupied while his parents dressed for church. Since these accidents happen in the safest environments, parents need to take specific note of the environment when someone keeps watch over so many children. You cannot take chances on what might happen in a home or center where the steps are unguarded, electric plugs are not covered, and cleaning materials are within easy reach of very busy children. Look long and hard at the safety of the child care environment, and then survey the types of equipment and toys the children have around them. If the children are in a safe place, and if they have many things to keep them busy, one person can keep track of a number of toddlers.

Is outside play important for toddlers? Our center has a big backyard with a lot of play equipment, but it seems like the teachers think it is too much trouble to get the children into coats and out of the door.

A pediatrician answered this question for you when he said that all children need to get outside several times every day, even in bitter cold weather. Licensing regulations usually require a minimum of an hour outside for centers operating more than five and one-half hours a day. The change in the air is healthy for the lungs because colds and other childhood diseases incubate in hot rooms. Children thrive when they have the room to run and play outdoors. Getting children outside is just as important as feeding them, and wise caregivers know toddlers are more likely to eat well and nap willingly when they have outside play time.

One child day center we visited had toddlers sitting in a circle while the "teacher" tried to introduce colors and letters to the wiggling bunch, and next she asked them to recite the days of the week. Other parents are pleased that their children are taught such preschool skills. Is this appropriate for these children?

This is another instance of a center's management not knowing appropriate learning activities for very young children. There are many activities that help children develop an emerging sense of literacy, and these teachers need to have some training in what to do. Teachers in child day centers are poorly paid, and few have courses in child development or in human growth and development. Unfortunately, many center directors will buy a packaged curriculum and use it for all of their children. Publishers will print anything centers will buy, appropriate or not. Center directors should spend their funds on trade books instead of these prepackaged monthly units. Teachers should be reading to the children throughout the day, and the children need to be able to pick up books and look at them at any time. There should be stacks of scrap paper around with fat crayons and markers for scribbling. Toddlers need to sing nursery rhymes and chant fingerplays. These are the appropriate learning activities for toddlers.

What are my child care options for a toddler?

The options for toddler child care do not differ much from those offered for the infant age group. However, you consider different factors when you evaluate each type of placement when you are considering that placement for a toddler.

1. *A relative keeps the child.* Many parents consider this the ideal arrangement—mother, sister, brother, aunt or grandma keeps the toddler. This is usually the least expensive form of child care available, especially if the relative is willing to do it with little or no repayment. However, toddlers create a different set of needs and you must determine if continuing in a sitter arrangement is the best choice for your child. Specific things to note when you choose this kind of provider:

  a. You must have a backup available on a moment's notice in case the primary sitter gets sick, breaks a leg, or goes on vacation.
  b. Unless you keep very careful records of payment by check, you are unable to claim your income tax deduction for child care when you pay a relative. You must pay the employer's portion of social security deductions for them.
  c. It is harder to criticize a relative if you disapprove of some practice the relative has concerning your child. What a way to start a family argument!
  d. Is the relative physically capable of running after an active toddler?
  e. Is her house child-proofed? Are there blanks in the electric sockets and are the cabinets locked so that your investigating tyke will not get into medicines or poisonous fluids? Many grandmothers simply forget how fast a child can get into something that can injure him and how quickly he can escape into a busy street.
  f. Is the yard fenced to protect him during outdoor play, or is the home at least located on a quiet back street?

2. *Get a nannie.* Two young lawyers in the Washington, D.C. area advertised for a college-educated nanny for their children and offered an $18,000 starting salary. There was also a recent story in *The New York Times* (April 14, 1993) about how people pay nannies poorly (national average is $200 to $250 a week) and take advantage of uneducated young women who have no training for other jobs. Those women were paid minimum wage and they worked twelve hours a day, seven days a week.

If you decide to get a nanny, do a good job of investigating your rights as well as your responsibilities. According to the *Times* article, federal law requires nannies be paid minimum wage—$4.25—and allows employers to deduct a small fee for room and board which in New York equals $6.15 per day. You must pay social security and unemployment taxes in addition.

There are many schools that claim to train nannies with the proper child-rearing information to provide parents with a peace of mind while they are at work. In actuality, many nannies are foreign-born young women who are looking for an adventure living abroad or for an opportunity to attend night classes while working, and they trade off sitting with your children for their room and board in this country. If you are interested in a "live-in" sitter, contact one of the nannie agencies for more information on the costs. Nannies generally have full responsibility for the children in their care but are not necessarily housekeepers, also. Many live in the home and receive room and board as the major part of their salaries. They offer an international flavor to child care and may even teach your child another language. Specific things to note when you choose this kind of provider:

   a. Contracts are usually for one year. Some people find they are changing nannies rather frequently.
   b. Unless you go through an agency that does the criminal checks and investigates references, you may be buying an unknown quality of service.
   c. You must file the forms with the IRS and pay employer's share in order to take your child care tax break. Make sure your nannie has a green card if she is not a U. S. citizen.
   d. You need an instant backup for those days your nannie is off or ill.
   e. Make sure your nannie is physically capable of keeping up with your active toddler.

3. *Get a sitter to come to your home each day.* This is a wonderful option because it means the toddler stays in familiar surroundings, sleeps in his own bed, and has very little change in his daily routine. Many sitters who come in for the day will also perform light housekeeping chores, and even fix dinner for the family. Specific things to note when you choose this kind of provider:

   a. In-home sitters are hard to find, and they want to be paid more than minimum wage if housekeeping chores are added to their job description. Many will actually refuse to sit with toddlers because they are so active.
   b. You must file IRS papers and pay social security fees.
   c. You need a backup for days when the sitter is sick or unavailable.

    d. You can require the sitter to have a criminal check through the state police so that you will know she has no record of abusive behavior.

4. *Take your child to the home of someone who takes care of several children in her home.* This category of sitter needs to be divided into two subcategories. One group of family child caretakers is unlicensed, unregulated and therefore generally cheaper than the other group.

In the Baby-Sitter's Home—the Unlicensed Sitter

There are many ads in newspapers soliciting parents to keep children at the sitter's home. Most of these are reputable baby-sitters. Depending upon the state in which you live, many of these sitters are subject to no regulations pertaining to fire safety, personal health standards, criminal checks, or required reference checks. You must ascertain this information yourself. Ask a prospective sitter if you can visit in her home for a morning to see how the day goes for the children in her care. Be aware that one person cannot care for a large group of toddlers with any degree of quality care, and this is why licensed homes must not exceed a maximum number of children per adult caretaker.[2] Check whether there is any type of record keeping for how often diapers are changed and medicine is given, or times when the child is fed. Does the sitter have cots for each of the children she is keeping? If not, will your child share a bed with other children? Is there an emergency backup sitter in case of the sitter's illness, or will that be your responsibility? Specific things to note when you choose this kind of provider:

    a. These sitters are usually reasonably priced and may request that you pay them in cash so that they do not have to report their income. You forfeit your IRS child care deduction if you agree to go along with this payment plan, and you are breaking the law.

    b. Be cautious when selecting this type of sitter because there are no controls whatsoever to insure your child against physical or sexual abuse. Regulatory agencies have no jurisdiction in these homes.

    c. Many of these sitters are well-educated mothers (often former teachers) who choose to sit for other children in order to stay home with their own children. These can be excellent placements if

---

2. For instance, in Virginia one adult is required for every five children for children ages 16 months to two years effective November, 1993.

carefully researched and if you make visits into the home prior to selecting them. Ask them what they will feed your toddler, and notice their disciplinary actions. Back off from sitters who yell and scream at their own children.

   d. It is a better social situation for a toddler if there are other children about her age, or a little older in the child care situation. She is ready to learn to take care of her own needs and she needs good models.

   e. Look for a sitter with a fenced-in back yard or a home on a little travelled street. Your toddler will need a lot of outdoor play time and you want it to be a safe time.

Licensed Family Day-Care Homes

There are several ways homes can fall under this category. They may be homes that have voluntarily registered with state regulatory agencies or with resource and referral agencies that provide oversight. They may be homes that have joined a family day-care system. The family day-care systems regulate/supervise the homes, provide bookkeeping services to permit patrons IRS deductions and to allow the sitters to meet filing requirements, and they help the sitters by referring clients to them. Specific things to note when you choose this kind of provider:

   a. Family day-care systems often maintain backup homes for substitute sitting when the primary sitter is ill.

   b. The system trains the sitters in child care procedures, health regulations, nutrition guidelines for lunches and snacks, and inservices them in different human growth and development issues that prepare them better for the job they undertake.

   c. The system will also give their providers training in disciplinary tactics, play options, arts and crafts activities, and first aid.

   d. The systems charge fixed rates, bill regularly, and provide documentation for your IRS child care deduction. You can voice complaints to them and expect a response from them.

5. *Child day centers.* The final option open to parents of children in the toddler category is the child day center. Many centers require children to be potty trained before they will enroll them. Licensing is very strict for these types of centers in most states, although some states still do not require church-operated centers to meet licensing regulations. You must

seek out those centers that accept toddlers. When you confirm that the center you are visiting is licensed, then you know a great deal about the physical environment your child will experience. Licensing requires providers to pass environmental tests such as holding asbestos-free certificates, making lead tests of the paint in the rooms, tests of the purity of the water, and even tests of the soil on the playground. Fire protection equipment, exits, alarms, and training are required. Even the water temperature at sinks is checked to be certain children cannot be accidentally scalded.

What licensing does not tell you is the kind of atmosphere your child will be experiencing. Does the center have a policy about allowing children to bring toys or other "comfort" items such as special teddies and old blankets? There is one center that refused to let children bring anything in because those items were not sterile. That center created its own sterile environment in which many toddlers cried themselves to sleep because they did not have their "blankie." Specific things to note when you choose this kind of provider:

   a. Remember that any business person can open a child day center, and knowledge of children's growth and development is not a requirement for licensing. Make sure your toddler is not just a figure on someone's profit and loss sheet.
   b. What kind of food and snacks does the center serve? Are these things your child will eat and enjoy? Does the center follow the U.S.D.A. rules on the use of 100% juice and some meals from the four food groups? Beware of unhealthy food choices and highly sugared powdered drinks.
   c. Is there a separate area for sick children, or must you keep your child at home every time he has a runny nose?

6. *Employer-sponsored child day centers.* This is an exciting new trend in child care. Basically, a company or corporation realizes that absenteeism is greatest among young parents, and that an effective way to reduce that rate is to participate in providing quality child care for its employees. Some companies set up their own licensed centers on their premises. They are like most licensed centers with the one important exception that the location allows parents to visit their children during the day, and parents can even join their children for lunch. Toddlers particularly enjoy knowing that mom or dad is nearby, and in case of a bad fall, the parent can be called to offer comfort. Mom and/or dad can join the

children for lunch frequently. These centers are usually subsidized by the company and this allows very affordable child care. Another way companies can participate involves the company purchasing slots in regular child day centers and reserving those slots for its employees. Frequently, these slots are subsidized to lower the employees' child care costs. One other benefit that companies provide is a payroll deduction of pretax dollars which the employee can use to pay child care costs. This reduces the costs for the employee. Contact your employer to see if any of these benefits are available to you.

Are there any part-time options for caring for toddlers?

There are a number of half-day tuition programs in most communities. These are not designed to provide child care, but to provide the socialization and group orientation many parents are seeking for their children in an early preschool setting. These programs were set up originally as preschool experiences for four- and five-year-olds. Now all fifty states have introduced some form of public school education for kindergartners within the past ten years, and those half-day programs now gear their classes to two-, three-, and four-year-olds. They distinguish between the age groups by offering different attendance options for each group. Most have a five-day program for the four-year-olds, a two- or three-day school experience for the three-year-olds, and in a limited number of programs, a two-day program for two-year-olds. Parents need to remember that a child has multiple years of schooling ahead, and most two-year-olds do not need a formal schooling experience.

If you do elect to send your young child to one of these half-day programs, a two-day-a-week session would be more advisable. One little girl, Morgan, attended a two-day program all year, and she adjusted to the school setting beautifully. She is the youngest of three very verbal children, and she thrived with a school experience of her own to share within her family. Another little girl may want to do anything else in the world before she wants to go to school at age two. Toddlers are very dependent on their moms, and they enjoy playing around the house with them near. They are very concerned about what is happening at home when they are not there. The vocabulary of children in this age group develops just as well, or better, than that of children in the two-year-old programs if adults in the home read to them. There are many years left to work on their socialization skills.

Finally, whatever type of child care you decide to select for your child, consult the center checklists in the appendix for specific things to note when you make a visit, and review the questions in the appendix that I am suggesting you ask of any prospective caregiver. Many parents feel embarrassed about asking providers questions such as, "Do you follow the U.S.D.A. guidelines for snacks and meals?" Since reasonable child care is very difficult to find, parents are afraid of angering a prospective baby-sitter by asking questions.

Your child's health and welfare is a very serious business, however, and if you do not determine ahead of time that a provider has no criminal record, it will be too late after you find your child was abused. Remember, if a provider will not allow you to visit, ask questions, and observe his/her program, scratch that provider off your list. There may be something in that program that the provider does not want you to observe.

SPECIAL NOTES AS YOU BEGIN YOUR SEARCH

1. When you begin visiting sitters or centers, go unannounced.
2. If you are not welcomed, drop that name from your list.
3. Check for cleanliness, licensing, posted menus, and a variety of play centers.
4. Do not be pressured into signing up on the same day you visit with such statements as, "We have only one opening, and if you do not sign up immediately, I won't be able to hold it for you."
5. Are you allowed to join your child at lunch on special occasions?
6. Can a toddler bring a special toy or a security blanket?
7. Licensed centers are required to have a parent's policy manual. Ask for a copy and take it home to study. This way you can find out their regulations regarding emergencies and sick children.

BOOKS FOR FURTHER READING

Elkind, David (1988). *The hurried child: Growing up too fast too soon.* New York: Addison-Wesley.

Elkind, David. (1987). Miseducation: Preschoolers at risk. New York: Knopf.

Katzev, Aphra R., & Bragdon, Nancy H. (1990). *Child care solutions: A parents' guide to finding child care you can trust.* New York: Avon.

Lusk, Diane, & McPherson, Bruce. (1992). *Nothing but the best: Making day care work for you and your child.* New York: Quill.

Chapter 4

THREE-YEAR-OLDS

Three-year-olds are wonderfully independent little people who are constantly on the go and eagerly learning new things at an amazing rate. They may be completely independent with that "do byself" approach to life, or they may still enjoy having their parents do everything for them. Some three-year-olds have fluent speech, and others are just beginning to move beyond the telegraphic speech stage where children communicate sparingly with phrases such as, "Me go" and "Daddy go work?" Three-year-old vocabularies range from 300 to 1000 words because there are no developmental guidelines that say when a child must talk fluently.

Children who are read to a great deal before age three usually demonstrate broad vocabularies, and they show an interest in the earliest stage of writing—scribbling. They recognize the big "M" over the local fast-food restaurant, and they can "read" the names on the cereal boxes that frequent your breakfast table. Their emergent literacy skills develop quickly as they become aware of the forms of environmental print they see daily. If encouraged, they "write" grocery lists before going to the store with you, and they recognize the printed letters that begin their names. Parents need to know that when they encourage these activities for three-year-olds, they are very instrumental in preparing the children to read several years down the road. Read to them, allow them to experiment with all kinds of paper and pens, pencils, and markers, and encourage them to retell stories you have read to them on a regular basis.

This is the age when many parents begin to feel their child needs some type of socialization in the outside world. This chapter reviews the three-year-old's schooling needs from two prospectives: the full-day child care facility, and the morning-out opportunities for two, three, and five days each week.

Programs are available for three-year-olds in more locations than for infants and toddlers. Many mothers opt to begin baby-sitting with other children when their own children reach this age. The children are more independent, they take direction more willingly, and they provide companionship for the sitter's own child or children. Licensed facilities can allow a higher number of children this age per "teacher," and this makes child care more profitable from a business viewpoint.[3] Diapering, bottle administering, and spoon feeding are not required for three-year-olds, and this makes the care process less complicated. The single common requirement for most programs is that the three-year-old child must be potty trained and able to care for himself independently. What are some typical questions that parents of three-year-olds are asking?

My three-year-old is really bored when her brother is at school. Is she too young to go to preschool?

There are many half-day programs available for three-year-olds. Visit several of these and determine if you think your child would enjoy participating in those types of activities. However, if you enroll your three-year-old and she begins to cry and complain about going to school, back off a bit. That child has thirteen formal years of schooling (K–12) ahead of her, and you do not want to jeopardize the whole educational experience by rushing her out of your home. The most successful preschool for three-year-olds is usually a two-day or three-day half-day program which allows her the best of both worlds—time with mother at home, and time to socialize with her friends at school.

My three-year-old is an only child and he does not know how to play with other children. Will a preschool teach him how to play?

Group play can be influential in teaching children the social rules of getting along with other children. It can be a disaster, however, if the people in charge do not facilitate the child's introduction into group activities. Some children need the careful instructional patter about sharing, taking turns, and trying different activities. If a shy child is dumped into a large group room or playground where very little supervision occurs, he learns only about bullies and unfair play practices. Visit any preschool you consider, and stay long enough to observe what goes on during *free play* periods. How much structure is available? Are some children allowed to tromp over others with little more interference from the teacher than an occasional, "Now, Susie!"? Children do learn to handle these situations themselves, but their initial ventures into group

---

3. For instance, for children ages two years to four years, Virginia requires one adult for every 10 children. This ratio varies from state to state.

activities are more successful when teachers initiate joint activities and guide the behavior of the group toward socially acceptable paths.

> *My sitter keeps the TV on all of the time and the children in her care watch cartoons and videos for hours on end. I know this is not good, but I don't know whether it is serious enough to change sitters.*

A recent news release from the National Assessment of Educational Progress study (September 16, 1993) blamed excessive TV viewing for the rising numbers of non-readers in this country. Children who develop their TV viewing habits at a very early age are at risk for having problems in school. Talk to your sitter and explain your concerns. Ask her to cut off the TV and read to the children. Offer to take a turn at visiting the library to boost her book collection. If she will not change this practice, you may want to find a placement where your child can develop other interests.

> *The teacher at our center called to tell me our three-year-old daughter bit another child. Shouldn't teachers handle problems like that at school and not bother parents at home?*

This is one of those questions that merit an "it all depends" answer. Is this the first time you have known your daughter to bite another child? Or have you had a problem with similar behavior at home? Teachers do handle misbehavior on the spot, at school, but when they notice repeated instances of behaviors that can hurt your child or other children, they contact the parents to share their concern. Most problems like this respond very well to a home and school united front. Your daughter demonstrated anger or frustration in a manner typical to three-year-olds. If she realizes that neither her teacher nor her family will accept that means of expressing herself, then it is likely that the behavior will cease. Support your teachers when they ask for your help.

> *What are some of the half-day options for three-year-olds?*

There are many more options for children who have become more independent than infants and toddlers. Many communities have church or community group sponsored Mother's Day Out programs. Mother gets to drop her child at the program one morning a week, and in return she helps with the program one day a month or every other month. There is little or no cost for participating in these programs. This allows mom to have a morning of childless activity, and it gives the three-year-old a chance to play with other children his age.

There are also a number of half-day tuition programs in most communities. These are not designed to provide child care but to provide the socialization, language development, and group orientation many parents seek for their children in a preschool setting. In the sixties these programs were set up as preschool experiences for four- and five-year-olds. Within the past ten years all fifty states introduced some form of public school education for kindergartners, and the half-day programs now gear their classes to three- and four-year-olds. The programs distinguish between the age groups by offering different attendance options for the fours and the threes. Most have a five-day program for the four-year-olds, and a two- or three-day school experience for the three-year-olds.

If you do elect to send your three-year-old child to one of these programs, the two- or three-day-a-week session is best. Children this age are still dependent on their moms, and they enjoy being around the house with them. They are very concerned about what is happening at home when they are not there. If three-year-olds are read to regularly and if they visit parks and museums, parents find their children's vocabularies develop just as well as those of children who attend three-year-old programs.

The benefits of a half-day program for three-year-olds are limited primarily to opportunities to gain socialization skills. They are introduced to listening in a group situation, to sharing toys, and to sharing an adult's attention. They receive early socialization into the mystique of schooling where standing in line, not talking out of turn, and doing what the teacher says is all important. Language development is another important benefit, but shy away from any program for three-year-olds that promises to teach the alphabet and numbers. If you see children sitting at tables and coloring work sheets, you will know you are in the wrong place. Too many three-year-olds are not ready for these activities, and forcing them to participate can turn them against school activities.

On the other hand, if you are away from home all day, and your caregiver does not understand the importance of reading books and talking with your child, then a preschool setting will be valuable. You know your child best, and you must weigh how well she will benefit from a program or how eager he is to go. Above all, if you enroll your child in a preschool program and he is obviously unhappy, do not hesitate for a moment to withdraw that child. Bear cubs may be ready to be independent when they are *three years old,* but many young children are not.

What are the full-day child care options for my three-year-old?

The options for child care do not differ much from those offered for the toddler age group. However, you consider different factors when you evaluate each type of placement when you are considering that placement for a three-year-old.

1. *A relative keeps the child.* Many parents consider this the ideal arrangement—mother, sister, brother, aunt or grandma keeps the child. This is usually the least expensive form of child care available, especially if the relative is willing to do it with little or no repayment. However, three-year-olds create a different set of needs and you must determine if continuing in a sitter arrangement is the best choice for your young child. Specific things to note when you choose this kind of provider:

   a. You must have a backup available on a moment's notice in case the primary sitter gets sick, breaks a leg, or goes on vacation.
   b. Unless you keep very careful records of payment by check, you are unable to claim your income tax deduction for child care when you pay a relative. You must also pay the employer's portion of social security deductions for them.
   c. It is harder to criticize a relative if you disapprove of some practice the relative has concerning your child. What a way to start a family argument!
   d. Is the relative physically capable of running after an active three-year-old?
   e. Is her house child-proofed—are there blanks in the electric sockets and are the cabinets locked so that your investigating child will not get into medicines or poisonous fluids? Many grandmothers simply have forgotten how fast a child can get into something that can injure him or how quickly he can escape into a busy street.
   f. Is the yard fenced to protect him during outdoor play, or is the home at least located on a quiet back street?
   g. Does the sitter have large motor skill toys to help his physical development such as jungle gyms, big wheels, and wagons?

2. *Get a nannie.* There are many schools that claim to train nannies with the proper child-rearing information to provide parents with peace

of mind while they are at work. In actuality, many nannies are foreign-born young women who are looking for an adventure living abroad or for an opportunity to attend night classes while working, and they trade off sitting with your children for their room and board in this country. If you are interested in a "live-in" sitter, contact one of the nannie agencies for more information on the costs. Nannies generally have full responsibility for the children in their care but are not necessarily housekeepers, also. Many live in the home and receive room and board as the major part of their salaries. They offer an international flavor to child care and may even teach your child another language. Specific things to note when you choose this kind of provider:

    a. Contracts are usually for one year. Some people find they are changing nannies rather frequently.
    b. Unless you go through an agency that does the criminal checks and investigates references, you may be buying an unknown quality of service unless you arrange for that check with the state police.
    c. You must file the forms with the IRS and pay employer's share in order to take your child care tax break. Make sure your nannie has a green card if she is not a U.S. citizen.
    d. You need an instant backup for those days your nannie is off or ill.
    e. Make sure your nannie is physically capable of keeping up with your active three-year-old.

3. *Get a sitter to come to your home each day.* This is a wonderful option because it means the child stays in familiar surroundings, sleeps in his own bed, and has very little change in his daily routine. Many sitters who come in for the day will also perform light housekeeping chores, and even fix dinner for the family. Specific things to note when you choose this kind of provider:

    a. In-home sitters are hard to find, and they want to be paid more than minimum wage if housekeeping chores are added to their job description.
    b. You must file IRS papers and pay social security fees.
    c. You need a backup for days when the sitter is sick or unavailable.
    d. You can require the sitter to have a criminal check through the state police so that you will know she has no record of abusive behavior.
    e. Make sure your caregiver understands the importance of reading

to your child frequently during the day. You will need to make sure that regular visits to the library keep her well supplied with books.

4. *Take your child to the home of someone who takes care of several children in her home.* This category of sitter needs to be divided into two subcategories. One group of family child caretakers is unlicensed, unregulated and therefore generally cheaper than the licensed group.

In the Baby-sitter's Home—the Unlicensed Sitter

There are many ads in newspapers soliciting parents to keep children at the sitter's home. Most of these are reputable baby-sitters. Depending upon the state in which you live, many of these sitters are subject to no regulations pertaining to fire safety, personal health standards, criminal checks, or required reference checks. You must ascertain this information yourself. Ask a prospective sitter if you can visit in her home for a morning to see how the day goes for the children in her care. Be aware that one person cannot care for a large group of children with any degree of quality care, and this is why licensed homes must not exceed a maximum number of children per adult caretaker. Check whether there is any type of record keeping for when medicine is given or times when the child is fed. Does the sitter have cots for each of the children she is keeping? If not, will your child share a bed with other children? Is there an emergency backup sitter in case of the sitter's illness, or will that be your responsibility? Specific things to note when you choose this kind of provider:

a. These sitters are usually reasonably priced and may request that you pay them in cash so that they do not have to report their income. You are forfeiting your IRS child care deduction if you agree to go along with this payment plan, and you are breaking the law.

b. Be cautious when selecting this type of sitter because there are no controls whatsoever to insure your child against physical or sexual abuse. Regulatory agencies have no jurisdiction in these homes in some states.

c. Many of these sitters are well-educated mothers (often former teachers) who choose to sit for other children in order to stay home with their own children. These can be excellent placements if

carefully researched and if you make visits into the home prior to selecting them. Ask them what they will feed your child, and notice their disciplinary actions. Back off from sitters who yell and scream at their own children.
- d. It is a better social situation for a three-year-old if there are other children about her age or a little older in the child care situation. She is ready to play with other children, and younger children will keep her from playing like a three-year-old.
- e. Make sure the sitter takes time to read to the children for whom she is caring and that there are books around for them to pick up and peruse.
- f. Look for a sitter with a fenced-in back yard or a home on a little travelled street. Your child will need a lot of outdoor play time and you want it to be a safe time. There should be equipment available to help strengthen the child's large muscle development. Things like jungle gyms, big wheels, and tricycles are important.

Licensed Family Day-Care Homes

There are several ways homes can fall under this category. They may be homes that have voluntarily registered with state regulatory agencies or with resource and referral agencies that provide oversight. They may be homes that have joined a family day-care system. The family day-care systems regulate/supervise the homes, provide bookkeeping services to permit patrons IRS deductions and to allow the sitters to meet filing requirements, and they help the sitters by referring clients to them. You can expect these homes to be more expensive than the unlicensed homes. Specific things to note when you choose this kind of provider:

- a. Family day-care systems often maintain backup homes for substitute sitting when the primary sitter is ill.
- b. The system trains the sitters in child care procedures, health regulations, nutrition guidelines for lunches and snacks, and inservices them in different human growth and development issues that prepare the sitters better for the job they have undertaken.
- c. The system will give their providers training in disciplinary tactics, play options, arts and crafts activities, and first aid.
- d. The systems charge fixed rates, bill regularly, and provide docu-

mentation for your IRS child care deduction. You can voice complaints to them and expect a response from them.

5. *Child day centers.* The final option open to parents of children in the three-year-old category is the child day center. Many centers require children to be potty trained before they will enroll them. Licensing is very strict for these types of centers in most states, although some states still do not require church-operated centers to meet licensing regulations. When you have confirmed that the center you are visiting is licensed, then you will know a great deal about the physical environment your child will be experiencing. Licensing requires providers to pass environmental tests such as holding asbestos-free certificates, making lead tests of the paint in the rooms, tests of the purity of the water, and even tests of the soil on the playground. Fire protection equipment, exits, alarms, and training are required. Even the water temperature at sinks is checked to be certain children cannot be scalded accidentally.

What licensing does not tell you is the kind of atmosphere your child will experience. Does the center have a policy about allowing children to bring toys or other "comfort" items such as special teddies and old blankets? There is one center that refused to let children bring anything in because those items were not sterile. That center created its own sterile environment in which many toddlers cried themselves to sleep because they did not have their "blankie." Specific things to note when you choose this kind of provider:

   a. Remember that any business person can open a day center, and knowledge of children's growth and development is not a requirement for licensing. Make sure your child is not just a figure on someone's profit and loss sheet.
   b. What kind of food and snacks does the center serve? Are these foods your child will eat and enjoy? Does the center follow the U.S.D.A. rules on the use of 100% juice and serve meals from the four food groups? Beware of unhealthy food choices and highly sugared powdered drinks.
   c. Is there a separate area for sick children, or must you keep your child at home every time he has a runny nose?

EMPLOYER–SPONSORED CHILD DAY CENTERS

This is an exciting new trend in child care. Basically, a company or corporation realizes that absenteeism is greatest among young parents, and that an effective way to reduce that rate is to participate in providing quality child care for its employees. Some companies set up their own licensed centers on their premises. They are like most licensed centers with the one important exception that the location allows parents to visit their children during the day, and parents can even join their children for lunch. Young children enjoy knowing that mom or dad is nearby, and in case of a bad fall, the parent can be called to offer comfort. Mom and/or dad can join the children for lunch frequently. Companies subsidize these centers and this allows very affordable child care. Companies participate also by buying slots in regular child day centers and then they reserve these slots for their employees. Frequently, the companies subsidize the cost of these slots to lower the employees' child care costs. One other widely used company benefit is to allow a payroll deduction of pretax dollars with which child care costs can be paid. This reduces child care costs for the employee. Contact your employer to see if any of these benefits are available to you.

Finally, whatever type of child care you decide to select for your child, do consult the center checklists in the appendix for specific things to note when you make a visit, and review the questions, too. Many parents feel embarrassed about asking providers questions such as, "Do you follow the U.S.D.A. guidelines for snacks and meals?" Since reasonable child care is difficult to find, parents are afraid of angering a prospective baby-sitter by asking questions.

Your child's health and welfare is a very serious business, however, and if you do not determine ahead of time that a provider has no criminal record, it will be too late after you find your child is abused. Remember, if a provider will not allow you to visit, ask questions, and observe his/her program, scratch that provider off your list. There may be something in that program that the provider does not want you to observe.

SPECIAL NOTES AS YOU BEGIN YOUR SEARCH

1. When you begin visiting sitters or centers, go unannounced.
2. If you are not welcomed, drop that name from your list.

3. Check for cleanliness, licensing, posted menus, a variety of play centers and many books.
4. Do not be pressured into signing up immediately with such statements as, "We have one opening, but I won't be able to hold it for you unless you sign up today."
5. Are you allowed to join your child at lunch on special occasions?
6. Ask if the child can bring a special toy or a security blanket.
7. Licensed centers are required to have a parent's policy manual. Ask for a copy and take it home to study. This way you can find out their regulations regarding emergencies and sick children.

BOOKS FOR FURTHER READING

Elkind, David. (1988). *The hurried child: Growing up too fast too soon.* New York: Addison-Wesley.

Elkind, David. (1987). *Miseducation: Preschoolers at risk.* New York: Knopf.

Katzev, Aphra R., & Bragdon, Nancy H. (1990). *Child care solutions: A parents' guide to finding child care you can trust.* New York: Avon.

Lusk, Diane, & McPherson, Bruce. (1992). *Nothing but the best: Making day care work for you and your child.* New York: Quill.

Chapter 5

FOUR-YEAR-OLDS

If you happen to meet a little girl with bright eyes, big ideas, and self-confidence to match, chances are she is a four-year-old. Children this age are wonderfully diverse human beings, but they share a cockiness that lets you know they think they are all grown up. They have an enthusiasm for life that is not matched. They are busily absorbing every bit of knowledge that comes their way via television, watching older children, and by listening to the grown-ups around them. For example, one four-year-old decided to build a lego city with her mom. Mom called it New York and then suggested they build a Sears Tower in the downtown area. The indignant young lady quickly set her mom straight with the admonition, "The Sears Tower isn't in New York, Mom, it's in Chicago!" The red-faced mom looked up at several adults in the room and asked, "Where did she learn that?" Where, indeed? The four-year-old is a sponge soaking up information from life around him at a rapid pace.

Many four-year-olds attend some type of preschool program. The Head Start program for disadvantaged children influenced many states to begin public school programs for four-year-olds. With the growth in the child care population, nearly eighty percent of the nation's four-year-olds are in some variety of classroom setting daily. Parents of the other twenty percent are looking for comparable experiences for their children. Their questions center on what type of preschool should they choose, how long a day is good for a four-year-old, and how many days a week their children should attend school. Here are several sample questions (and answers) that parents of four-year-olds ask:

My child doesn't like to sit still and listen to books. I know this is important, but I don't know how to force her to listen.

Most four-year-olds are already hooked on listening to stories, and the problem here may be that mom waited too late to introduce books. You can start pointing to animals and objects in picture books when children are very young—even six months old. That is a wonderful age to introduce books and to develop language. "See the cow? The cow says M–O–O!"

You must be inventive if you need to trick children into wanting to do something you know they will enjoy. For instance, the best time to begin reading to children who resist "sitting still to listen" is at bedtime. Begin a ritual where they can either go to bed, or you will read several stories to them. Use this as a wonderful together time when either mom or dad takes time out from a busy day to give some special time to the child through reading. The hours spent reading to your children are the best investment in time you can make.

Can I send my son to a five-day preschool program?
He really enjoys going to school.

Most four-year-olds do well in a five-day program, but there are some reasons to be concerned about them experiencing school burnout down the road. This youngster will *have* to go to school every day for the next thirteen years in his life. Never again will he have an opportunity to be at home all day on a regular basis, playing with his own toys, interacting with mom and his younger siblings. If you read several books to him every day, he will not be getting anything at school that he is not learning right there at home. While it does not hurt for him to go to preschool every day, he may be better off in the long run with a partial week schedule when it comes to maintaining his enthusiasm for going to school. If he attends two or three days a week, he will learn the things most public schools expect their children to know when they arrive in kindergarten—how to stand in line, to button their lips, to raise their hands for permission to talk, and to sit on their bottoms like quiet little Indians. The things he learns at home will be those values your family imparts. Once a child begins school, the family loses a great deal of control over what he sees, hears, and learns.

My daughter loves books and already knows most of the letters of the
alphabet. Shouldn't she attend a preschool that will teach her to read?

Parents need to remember that "knowing the letters of the alphabet" and understanding the concepts of sound and letter correlation are two different things. If the child is *really* ready to learn to read, you will not be able to stop her. Visit the kindergarten program your child will attend next year and find out what type of program she will get when she begins school. If the school system has adopted a developmentally appropriate approach for kindergarten instruction, then your daughter will benefit more from a preschool program that emphasizes play and developmentally appropriate activities. She will have many opportunities to write and read stories and her reading skills will be much stronger in the long run. If the kindergarten program is more academic in nature and demands that children entering kindergarten already know their letters and numbers, then you may want a four-year-old program that stresses learning that information.

Remember, however, that many preschool teachers are not certified to teach reading, and they do not understand the developmental processes involved in learning to read. The thing your daughter needs most is to have you read to her a great deal and to broaden her knowledge of the world at large. Children can read only those words for which they have an understanding. COW is just C–O–W until the child develops a sense of what that animal does, how it looks, and where it lives. Your best contribution to her readiness to read is to give her as many experiences as possible visiting farms, museums, zoos, bakeries, the beach, and the mountains. Recognizing the letters C–O–W and being able to write them will not be nearly as helpful to her comprehension of COW as patting the side of old Bessie at the state fair. FURCH has no meaning for you; you can pronounce it, you can write it, but you do not understand it. That nonsense word is a good example of why understanding what the word means is the most important facet of learning to read.

A good preschool will make your daughter "school wise" and will teach her those skills that make succeeding in the school arena a lot easier. Getting along with others, taking turns, listening carefully, and following directions are skills that will carry any student a whole lot further than just being able to recognize the letters of the alphabet.

> *My sitter is taking care of several two-year-olds and my daughter who is four. Does my child need to be with children her own age?*

The answer here depends completely on the number of hours a week your child is with the sitter. If your child is at the sitter's home forty hours a week and comes home to a family with no other older siblings, or neighborhood children her age, then you should be concerned that she is not developing the socialization skills children gain when they play with other children who are about their same age. Four-year-olds learn to lead, follow, compromise, finagle, and share when they are busily playing. The skills learned from playing only with two-year-olds are more along the lines of domineering, controlling, instructing, and mothering or nurturing—skills that do not necessarily help a child get along with her peers. Look at the number of hours each week the child plays with other children, and make your decision based on that information. Children need time to play with their peers.

My son is bored with preschool. He says they do the same old things every day. What can I do?

The first question to ask is whether this child is bored because he is tired of the preschool's activities, or does he dislike doing the tasks they require of him. There is a good chance he is asked to write, to color work sheets, and to memorize poems when he would rather be building blocks, steering trucks, or playing actively on the playground. The school he attends may not be following developmentally appropriate practices. Some preschools are so busy with their "academic" activities that they do not take the children outside to play.

This parent needs to talk with the preschool staff and let them help him identify whether his son is really bored or just not ready for the curriculum. If the school provides a "baby-sitting only" service where the children have unrestricted free play all day with little structure such as read-alouds and exploratory centers, then the boy can be bored. The curriculum and the boy's developmental age are both important in this parent's decision either to change schools or to decrease the number of days a week the child attends school.

Which is better for four-year-olds, a half-day or a full-day preschool program?

Many parents do not have this choice in programs because they are working and the child has to go the full day. However, where there is a choice, select a half-day program and ease the child into the school atmosphere. Children who attend these programs gain socialization skills, they enjoy new experiences through field trips, and they have opportunities to verbalize and enhance their language development. They are introduced to listening in a group situation, to sharing toys, and to sharing an adult's attention. They receive early socialization into the mystique of schooling where standing in line, not talking out of turn, and doing what the teacher says is all important.

If you do not elect to send your four-year-old child to one of these programs for five days each week, the three-day-a-week sessions are enough time for the child to get the benefits from the group and still feel a part of mom and life at home. If parents make sure their children are getting read to regularly, and if they take them on outings to visit parks and museums, their vocabularies develop just as well, or better than those of children in many five-day-a-week programs.

What are the half-day options for four-year-olds?

There are quite a few options in some communities. Here are some examples of half-day programs:

Mother's Day Out Programs. Many churches, community centers, and even neighborhood associations organize programs for young children. Mother gets to drop her child at the program one morning a week, and in return she helps with the program one day a month or every other month. There is little or no cost for participating in these programs. This allows mom to have a morning of childless activity, and it gives the four-year-old a chance to play with other children his age.

Head Start. Single parents and working mothers need to be aware of half-day opportunities such as Head Start in their communities. Head Start programs deal with all the needs of children, not just their need for schooling. They help parents find immunization facilities, counseling, good food, and well child checkups. Attendance in these programs is based on income, and the four-year-olds in families receiving Aid to Dependent Children, food stamps, or WIC funds are eligible for the Head Start program. Contact your local social services bureau for more information. Many families are eligible for Head Start and do not realize it. There is a widespread support to increase federal funding for the Head Start programs, and if this occurs, this type of program will become available to many more children.

Public School Programs. Many communities are starting four-year-old programs on-site at their public schools. These are offered to children who do poorly on preschool testing and are considered at-risk for school failure. However, many school districts are moving towards full-time educational programs for all children in their districts, and a call to your local school may uncover an opportunity for your four-year-old.

Church and Private School Programs. There are a number of half-day tuition programs in most communities. These are not designed to provide child care but to provide the socialization, language development, and group orientation many parents seek for their children in a preschool setting. These programs were set up originally as preschool experiences for four- and five-year-olds, but since all fifty states have introduced some form of public school education for kindergartners within the past ten years, the half-day private programs now gear their classes to three- and four-year-olds. The programs distinguish between the age groups by offering different attendance patterns for the fours and the threes. Most have a three- or five-day program for the four-year-olds, and a two- or three-day school experience for the three-year-olds. Your local Resource and Referral Center (see list in Appendix D) can give you a list of these schools in your community.

What are the full-day child care options for four-year-olds?

The options for child care do not differ much from those offered for the younger age groups. However, you should consider different factors when you evaluate each type of placement for the four-year-old:

1. *A relative keeps the child.* Many parents consider this the ideal arrangement—mother, sister, brother, aunt or grandma keeps the child. This is usually the least expensive form of child care available, especially if the relative is willing to do it with little or no repayment. However, four-year-olds create a different set of needs and you must determine if continuing in a sitter arrangement is the best choice for your child. Specific things to note when you choose this kind of provider:

   a. You must have a backup available on a moment's notice in case the primary sitter gets sick, breaks a leg, or goes on vacation.
   b. Unless you keep very careful records of payment by check, you are unable to claim your income tax deduction for child care when you pay a relative. You must pay the employer's portion of social security deductions for them.
   c. It is harder to criticize a relative if you disapprove of some practice the relative has concerning your child. What a way to start a family argument!
   d. Is the relative physically capable of running after an active four-year-old?
   e. Is the yard fenced to protect him during outdoor play, or is the home at least located on a quiet back street?
   f. Does the sitter have enough large motor skill toys to help your child's physical development such as jungle gyms, big wheels, and wagons?
   g. Does the sitter have other children around to play with? A four-year-old needs to play with other children.

2. *Get a nannie.* There are many schools that claim to train nannies with the proper child-rearing information to provide parents with peace of mind while they are at work. If you are interested in a "live-in" sitter, contact one of the nannie agencies for more information on the costs. Nannies generally have full responsibility for the children in their care, but they are not necessarily housekeepers. Many live in the home and receive room and board as the major part of their salaries.

Or get an "au pair." Many nannies are foreign-born young women called "au pairs" who look for an adventure living abroad or for an opportunity to attend night classes while working, and they trade off sitting with your children for their room and board in this country. They offer an international flavor to child care and may even teach your child another language. Specific things to note when you choose these types of provider:

  a. Contracts are usually for one year. Some people find they are changing nannies rather frequently.
  b. Unless you go through an agency that does the criminal checks and investigates references, you may be buying an unknown quality of service unless you arrange for that check with the state police.
  c. Unless you pay through the agency, you must file the forms with the IRS and pay employer's share in order to take your child care tax break. Make sure your au pair has a green card if she is not a U.S. citizen.
  d. You need an instant backup for those days your nannie is off or ill.
  e. Make sure your nannie is physically capable of keeping up with your active four-year-old.

3. *Get a sitter to come to your home each day.* This is a wonderful option because it means the child stays in familiar surroundings, sleeps in his own bed, and has very little change in his daily routine. Many sitters who come in for the day will also perform light housekeeping chores and even fix dinner for the family. Specific things to note when you choose this kind of provider:

  a. In-home sitters are hard to find, and they want to be paid more than minimum wage if housekeeping chores are added to their job description.
  b. You must file IRS papers and pay social security fees.
  c. You need a backup for days when the sitter is sick or unavailable.

d. You can require the sitter to have a criminal check through the state police so that you will know she has no record of abusive behavior.
e. Make sure your caregiver understands the importance of reading to your child frequently during the day. You will need to make sure that regular visits to the library keep her well supplied with books.
f. A sitter can transport your child to a half-day preschool program for you.

4. *Take your child to the home of someone who takes care of several children in her home.* This category of sitter needs to be divided into two subcategories. One group of family child caretakers is unlicensed, unregulated and therefore generally cheaper than the licensed group.

In the Baby-sitter's Home—the Unlicensed Sitter

There are many ads in newspapers soliciting parents to keep children at the sitter's home. Most of these are reputable baby-sitters. Depending upon the state in which you live, many of these sitters are subject to no regulations pertaining to fire safety, personal health standards, criminal checks, or required reference checks. You must ascertain this information yourself. Ask a prospective sitter if you can visit in her home for a morning to see how the day goes for the children in her care. Be aware that one person cannot care for a large group of children with any degree of quality care, and this is why licensed homes must not exceed a maximum number of children per adult caretaker. Check whether the sitter keeps any type of record for medicine given or for times when the child is fed. Does the sitter have cots for each of the children she is keeping? If not, must you provide one, or will your child share a bed with other children? Is there an emergency backup sitter in case of the sitter's illness, or will that be your responsibility? Specific things to note when you choose this kind of provider:

a. These sitters are usually reasonably priced and may request that you pay them in cash so that they do not have to report their income. You are forfeiting your IRS child care deduction if you agree to go along with this payment plan, and you are breaking the law.
b. Be cautious when selecting this type of sitter because there are no

controls whatsoever to insure your child against physical or sexual abuse. In many states regulatory agencies have no jurisdiction in these homes.

c. Many of these sitters are well-educated mothers (often former teachers) who choose to sit for other children in order to stay home with their own children. These can be excellent placements if carefully researched and if you make visits into the home prior to selecting them. Ask them what they will feed your child, and notice their disciplinary methods. Back off from sitters who yell and scream at their own children.

d. It is a better social situation for a four-year-old if there are other children about her age in the home. She needs to play like a four-year-old, and younger children will cause her to use less mature play strategies.

e. Make sure the sitter takes time to read to the children in her care, and confirm that there are books around for them to pick up and peruse.

f. Look for a sitter with a fenced-in back yard or a home on a little travelled street. Your child will need a lot of outdoor playtime and you want it to be a safe time. There should be equipment available to help strengthen the child's large muscle development. Things like jungle gyms, big wheels, and tricycles are important for four-year-olds.

Licensed Family Day-Care Homes

There are several ways homes can fall into this category. They may be homes that voluntarily register with state regulatory agencies or with resource and referral agencies that provide oversight. They may be homes that join a family day-care system. The family day-care systems supervise the homes, provide bookkeeping services to permit patrons IRS deductions and to allow the sitters to meet filing requirements, and they help the sitters by referring clients to them. You can expect these homes to be more expensive than the unlicensed homes. Specific things to note when you choose this kind of provider:

a. Family day-care systems often maintain backup homes for substitute sitting when the primary sitter is ill.

b. The system trains the sitters in child care procedures, health

regulations, nutrition guidelines for lunches and snacks, and inservices them in different human growth and development issues that prepare the sitters better for the job they have undertaken.
   c. The system will give their providers training in disciplinary tactics, play options, arts and crafts activities, and first aid.
   d. The systems charge fixed rates, bill regularly, and provide documentation for your IRS child care deduction. You can voice complaints to them and expect a response from them.

5. *Child day centers.* The final option open to parents of children in the four-year-old category is the child day center. Licensing is very strict for these types of centers in most states, although some states still do not require church-operated centers to meet licensing regulations. When you confirm that the center you are visiting is licensed, then you know a great deal about the physical environment your child will experience. Licensing requires providers to pass environmental tests such as holding asbestos-free certificates, making lead tests of the paint in the rooms, tests of the purity of the water, and even tests of the soil on the playground. Fire protection equipment, exits, alarms, and training are required. Even the water temperature at sinks is checked to be certain children cannot be scalded accidentally.

What licensing does not tell you is the kind of atmosphere your child will be experiencing. Specific things to note when you choose this kind of provider:
   a. Remember that any business person can open a child day center, and knowledge of children's growth and development is not a requirement for licensing. Make sure your child is not just a figure on someone's profit and loss sheet.
   b. What kind of food and snacks does the center serve? Are these things your child will eat and enjoy? Does the center follow the U.S.D.A. rules on the use of 100% juice and serve meals from the four food groups? Beware of unhealthy food choices and highly sugared powdered drinks.
   c. Is there a separate area for sick children, or must you keep your child at home every time he has a runny nose?

EMPLOYER-SPONSORED CHILD DAY CENTERS

This is an exciting new trend in child care. Basically a company or corporation realizes that absenteeism is greatest among young parents, and that an effective way to reduce that rate is to participate in providing quality child care for its employees. Some companies set up their own licensed centers on their premises. They are like most licensed centers with the important exceptions that the location allows parents to visit their children during the day and the fees are lower. Young children enjoy knowing that mom or dad is nearby, and in case of a bad fall, the parent can be called to offer comfort. Mom and/or dad can join the children for lunch frequently. These centers are usually subsidized by the company and this allows very affordable child care. Another way companies can participate involves the business buying slots in regular child day centers and reserving those slots for their employees. These slots are frequently subsidized to lower the employees' child care costs. One other company benefit that is becoming widely used is a payroll deduction of pretax dollars with which child care costs can be paid. This reduces child care costs for the employee. Contact your employer to see if any of these benefits are available to you.

Finally, whatever type of child care you decide to select for your child, do consult the center checklists in the appendix for specific things to note when you make a visit and review the questions to ask of any prospective caregiver. Many parents feel embarrassed about asking providers questions such as, "Do you follow the U.S.D.A. guidelines for snacks and meals?" Since reasonable child care is very difficult to find, parents are afraid of angering a prospective baby-sitter by asking questions. Your child's health and welfare is a very serious business, however, and if you do not determine ahead of time that a provider has no criminal record (for instance), it will be too late after you find your child was abused. Remember, if a provider will not allow you to visit, ask questions, and observe his/her program, scratch that provider off your list. There may be something in that program that the provider does not want you to observe.

SPECIAL NOTES AS YOU BEGIN YOUR SEARCH

1. When you begin visiting sitters or centers, go unannounced.
2. If you are not welcomed, drop that name from your list.

3. Check for cleanliness, licensing, posted menus, a variety of play centers and many books.
4. Do not be pressured into signing up immediately with such statements as, "We have one opening, but I won't be able to hold it for you unless you sign up today."
5. Are you allowed to join your child at lunch on special occasions?
6. Licensed centers are required to have a parent's policy manual. Ask for a copy and take it home to study. This way you can find out their regulations regarding emergencies and sick children.

BOOKS FOR FURTHER READING

Elkind, David. (1988). *The hurried child: Growing up too fast too soon.* New York: Addison-Wesley.

Elkind, David. (1987). *Miseducation: Preschoolers at risk.* New York: Knopf.

Katzev, Aphra R., & Bragdon, Nancy H. (1990). *Child care solutions: A parents' guide to finding child care you can trust.* New York: Avon.

Lusk, Diane, & McPherson, Bruce. (1992). *Nothing but the best: Making day care work for you and your child.* New York: Quill.

Chapter 6

FIVE-YEAR-OLDS

There are three or four very critical junctures in children's lives: when they start school, when they graduate from high school, when they graduate from college or elect a specific career path, and when they get married. The most important of these is the first—starting school. If children are to have happy, productive lives, they need to enjoy and do well at school. Each parent looks forward to a child beginning school with many different emotions and a great number of questions.

Thirty years ago children started to school when they turned six, now it is at age five. Unfortunately, each state establishes different deadlines for determining just when a five-year-old should begin school. For instance, Virginia changed from September 30 as the magic birth date to December 31 and back again to September 30 in just the past ten years. These deadlines mean that children begin school varying in age as much as twelve months. When the school doors open the day after Labor Day, some children are still four years old because they have late September birthdays, and others will turn six early in October. This birthday dilemma causes more soul-searching for parents of five-year-olds than any other single factor.

> *My son will not turn five until late August. Should I hold him out a year so that he will be more mature and more ready to start school?*

There are two answers to this question and large groups of educators who support each answer. One group will tell you that late birthday children are very immature and they need to grow a year before beginning school. They single out little boys as being particularly immature, and they recommend that parents "buy a year" for their sons by keeping them home one more year. Another group is just as determined to prove that younger, immature children are the very ones who most need to be at school.

Here are some things for you to think about before you try to find the answer. For instance, what does this mother mean by mature? Is she thinking of physical, social, cognitive, or emotional maturity? Is her son shy? clinging? very short? a loner? uninterested in books? or does he still expect her to do everything for him? The chances are good that this little boy is not immature in all of these facets of his development, and that every other child in kindergarten will be lagging in at least one of these developmental areas, too. Remember? Children all develop at different rates, and that is why developmentally appropriate practices are so important for school settings.

Next, the mother must find out what kind of kindergarten program her son will attend. If it is a very academic program that requires long periods of sitting at tables and writing letters and numbers, then a little boy who does not enjoy those types of activities will be in trouble. If, however, it is a developmentally appropriate kindergarten, then the teacher is going to allow that little boy to progress at his own developmental speed, and the choice of keeping him at home is inappropriate. He will be given every opportunity to mature at his own speed, and he will encounter new and exciting experiences every day.

The mother needs to consider, also, what her son will do during that extra year if he stays at home. Will he enjoy playing with the younger children? Will he really develop more maturity by being in a preschool classroom with children who are as much as a year younger than he is? If he is already more comfortable with children who are younger, and if he does not play with children his age when given a choice, then the year "out" may be a good choice. But, what will happen if six months into the school year this little boy suddenly blooms, becomes very verbal, begins directing all play opportunities, and gets a real hankering to learn letters and fool around with numbers? Is he going to become very bored with the younger children and the preschool activities? Unfortunately, none of us is equipped with a fortune-teller's crystal ball, and parents must make these decisions based on their best knowledge of their own children.

The type of kindergarten the child will attend is the key to making this decision easier: if the school is going to be academically demanding, then consider keeping him at home. If the school is using a developmentally appropriate curriculum, send him on. One other major factor can influence this decision, also. Is there a younger sibling who will be starting school next year? If holding this son out means he will be in the same grade as his brother or sister, then by all means send him to school and let him maintain his rank as the older brother in the family.

> *Our daughter is not old enough to enter kindergarten, but our school system allows children who just miss the birthday cutoff to take a test that permits them to enter kindergarten a year early. She passed the test, and now we must decide whether to send her or not. Any advice?*

This type of test usually measures how much a five-year-old already knows, what information she has mastered. Typically, schools ask the children to identify shapes, numbers, colors, and parts of the body; to understand terms such as above, below, under, and over; and to do things like pointing to the "first" and the "last" cars in a train. This is not testing their cognitive ability, just what they already know. This type of test does not predict how a child will do in school. It does tell you that the child is ready for school activities that require they know this type of information. The parents must decide whether this little girl is also socially, physically, and emotionally ready to start school. They should talk to their daughter's preschool teacher to see if she thinks the child is ready for kindergarten. They can watch her play with other five-year-olds and determine if she stands up for her rights, or if she lets them tromp on her. Does the child cry easily? Does she enjoy being away from home? Does she "read" books at every opportunity?

They need to remember, however, that when this child begins school she will certainly be the youngest in her class, and major decisions down the road will be affected by her age. She will be the last in her class to get her driver's license, she will want to start dating at a young age, just as she will want to begin wearing makeup and piercing her ears earlier. David Elkind's book, *The Hurried Child,* is good reading material for parents making this decision. Many children do very well in an accelerated placement when parents and teachers do not forget to remember how old they really are.

> *My daughter just took the kindergarten test, and the principal says she failed it because she couldn't draw circles and squares. I did not let her play with pencils and crayons much and she just needs that experience. Will the extra year of kindergarten (junior kindergarten) that they recommend help her at all?*

Educators contend that the development of children's writing skills corresponds closely with the development of their readiness for reading instruction. If your daughter attends a school program that has a very academic orientation, then she will need time to develop the eye/hand, letter/sound correlations that experience in using writing tools, retelling stories, and hearing many books read aloud affords her.

One little four-year-old, Dawn, never had experience with writing tools because her mom feared she would mark on the walls and tables. When Dawn took the kindergarten entrance test, she did poorly on the fine motor skills section. Since her birthday was in November, the school recommended she attend its junior kindergarten program. Seven years later she is in the fifth grade and reading in the top reading group at her school. Her self-esteem is good and she appears to have benefitted from her extra year. There are examples, too, of children who seem to struggle whether they get that extra year or not. This call for an extra year is a gamble, and parents must decide what is best for their own child. Do not compare him or her to any other children, because all children are uniquely different.

If your child just misses the birthday cutoff for attending kindergarten or if you have decided to keep her home for another year, there are some interesting alternatives for the young five-year-olds. If she attended a four-year-old preschool, hopefully it was just for three days a week, and the five-year-old can attend every day. Repeating the same program the child attended the year before is a bad idea, so you may want to switch school settings to get a program that will be different and varied for the child. You may want to broaden the range of activities in which your child participates: ballet, gymnastics, swimming, piano lessons, karate, and little league soccer, football and softball all cater to five-year-olds. Any *one* of these activities gives the child a special interest to develop, but does not overwhelm him.

Church and Private School Programs. There are a number of half-day tuition programs in most communities. These are not designed to provide child care but to provide the socialization, language development, and group orientation many parents seek for their children in a preschool setting. These programs were set up as preschool experiences for four- and five-year-olds originally, but since all fifty states introduced some form of public school education for kindergartners within the past ten years, those half-day programs gear their classes now to three- and four-year-olds. They distinguish between the age groups by offering different attendance patterns for the young fives, the fours and the threes.

If you do elect to send your young five-year-old child to one of these programs, the five-day-a-week sessions are a good choice. When children are read to regularly and when they visit parks and museums, their vocabularies develop just as well as those of children in kindergarten programs. They spend the year getting geared up for real school, and the benefits of these programs for young five-year-olds are the opportunities to gain socialization skills, experiences offered through field trips, and the chances to verbalize and enhance their language development. They improve their readiness for school by learning to function in group situations, learning to follow directions, and by acquiring those school skills such as raising their hands to talk, sitting on their bottoms like a quiet little Indian, and carefully paying attention to their teacher. They receive early socialization into the mystique of schools where standing in line, not talking out of turn, and doing what the teacher says is all important.

What are my full-day child care options for a five-year-old?

The options for child care do not differ much from those offered for the younger age groups. However, you should consider different factors when you evaluate each type of placement when you are considering that placement for a young five-year-old.

1. *A relative keeps the child.* Many parents consider this the ideal arrangement—mother, sister, brother, aunt or grandma keeps the child. This is usually the least expensive form of child care available, especially if the relative is willing to do it with little or no repayment. However, five-year-olds create a different set of needs and you must determine if continuing in a sitter arrangement is the best choice for your child. Specific things to note when you choose this kind of provider:

   a. You must have a backup available on a moment's notice in case the primary sitter gets sick, breaks a leg, or goes on vacation.
   b. Unless you keep very careful records of payment by check, you are unable to claim your income tax deduction for child care when you pay a relative. You must also pay the employer's portion of social security deductions for them.
   c. It is harder to criticize a relative if you disapprove of some practice the relative has concerning your child. What a way to start a family argument!
   d. Is the relative physically capable of running after an active five-year-old?

    e. Is the yard fenced to protect him during outdoor play, or is the home at least located on a quiet back street?
    f. Does the sitter have enough large motor skill toys to help your child's physical development such as jungle gyms, big wheels, and wagons?
    g. Are there other children around to play with? A five-year-old must play with others.

2. *Get a nannie.* There are many schools that claim to train nannies with the proper child-rearing information to provide parents with peace of mind while they are at work. In actuality, many nannies are foreign-born young women who are looking for an adventure living abroad or for an opportunity to attend night classes while working, and they trade off sitting with your children for their room and board in this country. If you are interested in a "live-in" sitter, contact one of the nannie agencies for more information on the costs. Nannies generally have full responsibility for the children in their care but are not necessarily housekeepers, also. Many live in the home and receive room and board as the major part of their salaries. They offer an international flavor to child care and may even teach your child another language. Specific things to note when you choose this kind of provider:

    a. Contracts are usually for one year. Some people find they are changing nannies rather frequently.
    b. Unless you go through an agency that does the criminal checks and investigates references, you may be buying an unknown quality of service unless you arrange for that check with the state police.
    c. You must file the forms with the IRS and pay employer's share in order to take your child care tax break. Make sure your nannie has a green card if she is not a U.S. citizen.
    d. You need an instant backup for those days your nannie is off or ill.
    e. Make sure your nannie is physically capable of keeping up with your active five-year-old.

3. *Get a sitter to come to your home each day.* This is a wonderful option because it means the child stays in familiar surroundings, sleeps in his own bed, and has very little change in his daily routine. Many sitters who come in for the day will also perform light housekeeping chores and even fix dinner for the family. Specific things to note when you choose this kind of provider:

a. In-home sitters are hard to find, and they want to be paid more than minimum wage if housekeeping chores are added to their job description.
b. You must file IRS papers and pay social security fees.
c. You need a backup for days when the sitter is sick or unavailable.
d. You can require the sitter to have a criminal check through the state police so that you will know she has no record of abusive behavior.
e. Make sure your caregiver understands the importance of reading to your child frequently during the day. You will need to make sure that regular visits to the library keep her well supplied with books.

4. *Take your child to the home of someone who takes care of several children in her home.* This category of sitter needs to be divided into two subcategories. One group of family child caretakers is unlicensed, unregulated and therefore generally cheaper than the licensed group.

In the Baby-Sitter's Home—the Unlicensed Sitter

There are many ads in newspapers soliciting parents to keep children at the sitter's home. Most of these are reputable baby-sitters. Depending upon the state in which you live, many of these sitters are subject to no regulations pertaining to fire safety, personal health standards, criminal checks, or required reference checks. You must ascertain this information yourself. Ask a prospective sitter if you can visit in her home for a morning to see how the day goes for the children in her care. Be aware that one person cannot care for a large group of children with any degree of quality care, and this is why licensed homes must not exceed a maximum number of children per adult caretaker.[4] Check whether there is any type of record keeping for when medicine is given or times when the child is fed. Does the sitter have cots for each of the children she is keeping? If not, will your child share a bed with other children? Is there an emergency backup sitter in case of the sitter's illness, or will that be your responsibility? Specific things to note when you choose this kind of provider:

a. These sitters are usually reasonably priced and may request that you pay them in cash so that they do not have to report their

---

4. For instance, Virginia allows one adult to every 12 children ages four to school age (five by September 30). At school age it becomes one adult to every 20 children.

income. You are forfeiting your IRS child care deduction if you agree to go along with this payment plan, and you are breaking the law.

b. Be cautious when selecting this type of sitter because there are no controls whatsoever to insure your child against physical or sexual abuse. Regulatory agencies have no jurisdiction in these homes.

c. Many of these sitters are well-educated mothers (often former teachers) who are choosing to sit for other children in order to stay home with their own children. These can be excellent placements if carefully researched and if you make visits into the home prior to selecting them. Ask them what they will feed your child, and notice their disciplinary actions. Back off from sitters who yell and scream at their own children.

d. It is a better social situation for a five-year-old if there are other children about her age. She needs to play like a five-year-old, and younger children will cause her to use less mature play strategies.

e. Make sure the sitter takes time to read to the children for whom she is caring and that there are books around for them to pick up and peruse. You do not want them playing Nintendo and other video games for hours on end.

f. Look for a sitter with a fenced-in backyard or a home on a little travelled street. Your child will need a lot of outdoor playtime and you want it to be a safe time. There should be equipment available to help strengthen the child's large muscle development. Things like jungle gyms, big wheels, and tricycles are important.

Licensed Family Day-Care Homes

There are several ways homes can fall into this category. They may be homes that have voluntarily registered with state regulatory agencies or with resource and referral agencies that provide oversight. They may be homes that have joined a family day-care system. The family day-care systems regulate/supervise the homes, provide bookkeeping services to permit patrons IRS deductions and to allow the sitters to meet filing requirements, and they help the sitters by referring clients to them. You can expect these homes to be more expensive than the unlicensed homes. Specific things to note when you choose this kind of provider:

a. Family day-care systems often maintain backup homes for substitute sitting when the primary sitter is ill.

    b. The system trains the sitters in child care procedures, health regulations, nutrition guidelines for lunches and snacks, and inservices them in different human growth and development issues that prepare the sitters better for the job they have undertaken.
    c. The system will also give their providers training in disciplinary tactics, play options, arts and crafts activities, and first aid.
    d. The systems charge fixed rates, bill regularly, and provide documentation for your IRS child care deduction. You can voice complaints to them and expect a response from them.

5. *Child day centers.* The final option open to parents of children in the young five-year-old category is the child day center. Licensing is very strict for these types of centers in most states, although some states still do not require church-operated centers to meet licensing regulations. When you have confirmed that the center you are visiting is licensed, then you will know a great deal about the physical environment your child will be experiencing. Licensing requires providers to pass environmental tests such as holding asbestos-free certificates, making lead tests of the paint in the rooms, tests of the purity of the water, and even tests of the soil on the playground. Fire protection equipment, exits, alarms, and training are required. Even the water temperature at sinks is checked to be certain children cannot be scalded accidentally.

What licensing does not tell you is the kind of atmosphere your child will be experiencing. Specific things to note when you choose this kind of provider:

    a. Remember that any business person can open a child day center, and knowledge of children's growth and development is not a requirement for licensing. Make sure your child is not just a figure on someone's profit and loss sheet.
    b. What kind of food and snacks does the center serve? Are these things your child will eat and enjoy? Does the center follow the U.S.D.A. rules on the use of 100% juice and serve meals from the four food groups? Beware of unhealthy food choices and highly sugared powdered drinks.
    c. Is there a separate area for sick children, or must you keep your child at home every time he has a runny nose?

EMPLOYER-SPONSORED CHILD DAY CENTERS

This is an exciting new trend in child care. Basically, a company or corporation realizes that absenteeism is greatest among young parents, and that an effective way to reduce that rate is to participate in providing quality child care for its employees. Some companies set up their own licensed centers on their premises. They are like most licensed centers with the one important exception that the location allows parents to visit their children during the day, and parents can even join their children for lunch. Young children enjoy knowing that mom or dad is nearby, and in case of a bad fall, the parent can be called to offer comfort. Mom and/or dad can join the children for lunch frequently. These centers are usually subsidized by the company and this allows very affordable child care. Other participation by companies involves their buying slots in regular child day centers and reserving those slots for their employees. These slots are frequently subsidized to lower the employees' child care costs. One other company benefit that is becoming widely used is a payroll deduction of pretax dollars with which child care costs can be paid. This reduces child care costs for the employee. Contact your employer to see if any of these benefits are available to you.

Finally, whatever type of child care you decide to select for your child, do consult the center checklists in the Appendix for specific things to note when you make a visit and also review the questions that I am suggesting you ask of any prospective caregiver. Many parents feel embarrassed about asking providers questions such as, "Do you follow the U.S.D.A. guidelines for snacks and meals?" Since reasonable child care is very difficult to find, parents are afraid of angering a prospective baby-sitter by asking questions.

Your child's health and welfare is a very serious business, however, and if you do not determine ahead of time that a provider has no criminal record (for instance), it will be too late after you find your child was abused. Remember, if a provider will not allow you to visit, ask questions, and observe his/her program, scratch that provider off your list. There may be something in that program that the provider does not want you to observe.

SPECIAL NOTES AS YOU BEGIN YOUR SEARCH

1. When you begin visiting sitters or centers, go unannounced.
2. If you are not welcomed, drop that name from your list.
3. Check for cleanliness, licensing, posted menus, a variety of play centers and many books.
4. Do not be pressured into signing up immediately with such statements as, "We have one opening, but I won't be able to hold it for you unless you sign up today."

5. Are you allowed to join your child at lunch on special occasions?
6. Licensed centers are required to have a parent's policy manual. Ask for a copy and take it home to study. This way you can find out their regulations regarding emergencies and sick children.

BOOKS FOR FURTHER READING

Elkind, David. (1988). *The hurried child: Growing up too fast too soon.* New York: Addison-Wesley.

Elkind, David. (1987). *Miseducation: Preschoolers at risk.* New York: Knopf.

Katzev, Aphra R., & Bragdon, Nancy H. (1990). *Child care solutions: A parents' guide to finding child care you can trust.* New York: Avon.

Lusk, Diane, & McPherson, Bruce. (1992). *Nothing but the best: Making day care work for you and your child.* New York: Quill.

Chapter 7

PROBLEMS FOR FAMILIES SEEKING CHILD CARE

There are several major hurdles that some families must conquer when they look for child care. Parents whose children have special needs find out that they have a much harder time locating child care. This is also true for parents who work unusual schedules or shift work. Also, many families are just learning that there is a law that requires they pay social security and Medicare taxes for their sitters. These problems are discussed.

CHILDREN WITH SPECIAL NEEDS

Federal law guarantees a free and appropriate education for all handicapped youth in a variety of specially designed programs. This instruction is available in the public school sector for children ages 2–21 inclusive, who are emotionally disturbed, have impaired vision, speech or hearing, are learning disabled, or who are mentally or physically handicapped. Many school districts provide programs also for preschool children whose disabilities are not specifically identified. The major task here is to get parents who suspect their children are developmentally delayed, or who are in any way handicapped, to seek the services provided by the public school systems. Many preschool teachers are helpful in getting this type of information to parents.

Hunter, a four-year-old, attended a church-operated preschool three mornings a week. His teacher called his parents in for a conference about midyear to tell them that Hunter was not joining in the group activities and that his motor skills lagged behind those of the other children in the group. Soon after that, his mother noticed an advertisement in the local paper for preschool screening test dates in her local school district, and she arranged to have Hunter tested. When his testing showed significant developmental delays, the school system put him in a five-day-a-week half-day program where he received special educational services such as occupational therapy for his motor delays. The following fall he went to the regular half-day kindergarten program offered by his school district in the mornings, and in the afternoon he continued with the special education program. He made tremendous strides during the year and he attended a regular first grade program the next fall. The experiences at the preschool level made Hunter's chances of success at school much stronger than they would have been if his preschool teacher had ignored his behavior.

Help is available, typically on a half-day basis, for learning-delayed and handicapped children. Unfortunately, many parents have a great deal of trouble finding full-time child care for their children who have special needs. Many child day centers refuse to accept children with severe handicaps or emotional problems. They will tell you that they accept children on a case-by-case basis, but you will not find handicapped children among their students. Current programs for children needing special educational placements stress the advantages for the handicapped children and the "regular" children when the school includes the special needs children in the regular classroom.

Mattie is a four-year-old who was born with malformed legs. She attended a preschool handicapped class in the mornings getting about her classroom with the use of a walker; she could not walk and she was not toilet trained. Many of the other children in her class used walkers to move around. A special child day center opened midyear that encouraged handicapped children to attend, so Mattie rode a school bus at noon every day to be dropped off at the child day center for the afternoon session. Here she encountered other children her age, but none of them used a walker or wore diapers. They climbed jungle gym bars and careened about the blacktop on hot wheels.

Within three months Mattie was walking on her poorly shaped feet and joining in most of the activities with the other children; her toilet training was nearly completed. Mattie is a good example of why handicapped children need to be included in regular classroom settings as often as possible. Surrounding Mattie with children who did not have disabilities made her want to keep up with their activities. As long as she worked and played with handicapped youngsters, she saw no need to walk.

How can I find a child care placement that will accept my handicapped child?

Many communities have resource and referral centers set up to answer child care questions that parents ask. Call your nearest center and hope that ongoing educational attempts by such organizations as the National Association for Early Childhood Education (NAEYC) and the National Association of Child Care Resource and Referral Agencies encouraged child day centers in your area to accept handicapped youngsters. There is a list of state centers for resource and referral agencies in the Appendix. Your state center can direct you to centers in your locale.

Many small center operators feel ill equipped to manage the care of handicapped children. Check with your local social service agency to find out if your state has organizations such as *Project Daniel* that provide aides to accompany children with special needs. Some children need an aide's ears or eyes to help them get along in the classroom with the other children, and these agencies provide aides or train aides to help out. If your child qualifies for such assistance, then the aide accompanies your child to the child day center and teaches the center personnel how to include him in its daily activities.

> *My child is just three years old. How am I supposed to know if he has some handicapping disability that will keep him from learning?*

Most pediatricians are quick to help spot problem areas in their young patients, but you will notice ways in which your particular child differs from the average three-year-old in behavior and physical aptitude before the doctor does. Be sure to consult with him as soon as you feel any concern about the growth and development of your child.

There are many different ways in which a child can be handicapped. The term, *handicapping conditions,* encompasses a large list of problems that affect children. Here is a typical listing of possible handicapping conditions copied directly from a legal notice, the CHILD FIND STATEMENT, published in a local paper:

(1) "Autism" means a developmental disability significantly affecting verbal and nonverbal communication and social interaction, generally evident before age 3, that adversely affects a child's educational performance. Other characteristics often associated with autism are engagement in repetitive activities and stereotyped movements, resistance to environmental change or change in daily routines, and unusual responses to sensory experiences. The term does not apply if a child's educational performance is adversely affected primarily because the child has a serious emotional disturbance, as defined in paragraph (b) (9) of this section.

(2) "Deaf-Blindness" means concomitant hearing and visual impairments, the combination of which causes such severe communication and other developmental and educational problems that they cannot be accommodated in special education programs solely for children with deafness or children with blindness.

(3) "Deafness" means a hearing impairment that is so severe that the child is impaired in processing linguistic information through hearing, with or without amplification, that adversely affects a child's educational performance.

(4) "Hearing Impairment" means an impairment in hearing, whether permanent or fluctuating, that adversely affects a child's educational performance.

(5) "Mental Retardation" means significantly subaverage general intellectual functioning existing concurrently with deficits in adaptive behavior and manifested during the developmental period that adversely affects a child's educational performance.

(6) "Multiple Disabilities" means concomitant impairments (such as mental retardation-blindness, mental retardation-orthopedic impairment, etc.), the combination of which causes such severe educational problems that they cannot be accommodated in special education programs solely for one of the impairments. The term does not include deaf-blindness.

(7) "Orthopedic Impairment" means a severe orthopedic impairment adversely affects a child's educational performance. The term includes impairments caused by congenital anomaly (e.g., clubfoot, absence of some member, etc.), impairments caused by disease (e.g., poliomyelitis, bone tuberculosis, etc.), and impairments from other causes (e.g., cerebral palsy, amputations, and fractures or burns that cause contractures).

(8) "Other Health Impairments" means having limited strength, vitality or alertness, due to chronic or acute health problems such as a heart condition, tuberculosis, rheumatic fever, nephritis, asthma, sickle cell anemia, hemophilia, epilepsy, lead poisoning, leukemia, or diabetes that adversely affects a child's educational performance.

(9) "Serious Emotional Disturbance" is defined as follows:
   (i) The term means a condition exhibiting one or more of the following characteristics over a long period of time and to a marked degree that adversely affects a child's educational performance—

(a) An inability to learn that cannot be explained by intellectual sensory health factors;
(b) An inability to build or maintain satisfactory interpersonal relationships with peers and teachers;
(c) Inappropriate types of behavior or feelings under normal circumstances;
(d) A general pervasive mood of unhappiness or depression; or
(e) A tendency to develop physical symptoms or fears associated with personal or school problems.

(ii) The term includes schizophrenia. The term does not apply to children who are socially maladjusted, unless it is determined that they have a serious emotional disturbance.

(10) "Specific Learning Disability" means a disorder in one or more of the basic psychological processes involved in understanding or in using language, spoken or written, that may manifest itself in an imperfect ability to listen, think, speak, read, write, spell, or to do mathematical calculations. The term includes such conditions as perceptual disabilities, brain injury, minimal brain dysfunction, dyslexia, and developmental aphasia. The term does not apply to children who have learning problems that are primarily the result of visual, hearing or motor disabilities, of mental retardation, of emotional disturbance, or of environmental, cultural, or economic disadvantage.

(11) "Speech or Language Impairment" means a communication disorder such as stuttering, impaired articulation, a language impairment, or a voice impairment that adversely affects a child's educational performance.

(12) "Visual Impairment Including Blindness" means an impairment in vision that, even with correction, adversely affects a child's educational performance. The term includes both partial sight and blindness.

Once you have confirmed that your child has special needs, educate yourself on the child's condition and become familiar with the laws which guarantee that child specific services. Join advocate groups and support groups sponsored by local agencies. The child resource and referral agencies can give you leads to these agencies. If a child day center refuses your child, investigate whether they will accept him if you can furnish an aide to assist him in the classroom. Many of the operators of these centers are uninformed about special needs children and they fear taking responsibility for them.

Licensed centers are required to have wheelchair-accessible entry and bathroom facilities. They are your best bet for finding a center to care for your handicapped child.

PARENTS WHO WORK UNUSUAL HOURS

Some parents work very different schedules from the traditional nine to five day. This includes everyone who does shift work in the manufacturing industry, as well as personnel in public services such as police and fire fighters, store employees, and those who staff hospitals and nursing homes. Many mothers work part-time schedules and find it very difficult to locate child care for their children at these odd hours. Most child day centers require contractual obligations for a full week's wage whether the child attends each day or not. Additionally, those centers open after many of the shift workers have reported to work, and they close around 6 p.m.

For instance, Susan is a registered nurse in the labor and delivery unit at her local hospital. She works a part-time schedule in order to spend as much time as possible with her four- and six-year-old children. She reports to work for the 3–11 p.m. shift two days each week and every other weekend. She leaves home before her son's school bus has arrived. The local child day center closes at 6 p.m. and her husband cannot pick up the children there before 6:30 p.m., so the child day center is not an option. She needs someone to come in and care for her daughter, to meet the school bus, and to stay until her husband arrives at 7 p.m. Locating this type of child care has been a real nightmare for her. Most "sitters" want to quit at 6 p.m. in order to be at home to prepare dinner for their own families.

Susan found teenage sitters to be very undependable, and she had six different sitters one year. The sitters called up the night before to tell her they had something else to do the next day, or they quit the job with no notice. Both grandmothers live out of town, and no close family members live near Susan to help her out in emergency situations.

Other parents who work evening hours find it tough to find sitters who will be willing to feed the children dinner and help them with their homework. One mother finally arranged to pay her sitter $40 a week extra in order to get the sitter to read books to her children each night.

What are the options for parents who work part-time or who work on shifts?

Teenage Sitters

Teens are available because they are usually home from school in the early afternoon hours. If you hire a teenager to watch your children on a regular basis, treat the sitter as a regular employee. Write a contract with the teen that states the definite hours she/he is expected to work, what additional tasks (such as reading to the children nightly) you require, and set up definite procedures for paying them. Pay on an every two-week basis (when you get paid) and require a two-day notice for any missed time, or require her to provide her own substitute. Promise her a pay increase when she proves she can handle the responsibilities of the job well. You get what you pay for, and you should pay at least minimum wage to sitters who work for you on a regular schedule. Be sure to seek recommendations from other people for whom the teen has worked, and require a criminal records' check if the sitter is not known to you or to your neighbors.

Shift Sharing

You can advertise at your work location for a parent who works an opposite shift who would be interested in trading sitting responsibilities. You keep their children during their shift, and they keep yours for you. This will take some planning, but it is one more idea to try.

Employer-Sponsored Child Day Centers

Fortunately, hospitals and nursing homes have been the industry leaders in establishing child care for their shift workers. A local hospital or nursing home may have a center, and they will allow outsiders to use the facility if their own employees do not fill the slots. This type of care is perfect for shift workers, and for people with erratic schedules, because they are set up to handle children for these types of workers. Most hospital child day centers will have access to a sick ward and they take children who are sick.

This is an exciting new trend in child care. Basically, a company or corporation realizes that absenteeism is greatest among young parents, and that an effective way to reduce that rate is to participate in providing quality child care for its employees. Some companies set up their own licensed centers on their premises. They are like most licensed centers with the one important exception that the location allows parents to visit their children during the day, and parents with erratic schedules can join their children for breakfast or a bedtime story. Young children enjoy knowing that mom or dad is nearby, and in case of a bad fall, the parent can be called to offer comfort. These centers are usually subsidized by the company and this allows very affordable child care. Other participation by companies involves their buying slots in regular child day centers and reserving those slots for their employees. They barter with the centers to extend their hours for their employees' with special scheduling needs. These slots are frequently subsidized to lower the employees' child care costs. One other company benefit that is becoming widely used is a payroll deduction of pretax dollars with which child care costs can be paid. This reduces child care costs for the employee. Contact your employer to see if any of these benefits are available to you.

LEGAL AND TAX RESPONSIBILITIES FOR CHILD CARE

Most Americans are surprised to learn that families who hire babysitters are required to pay federal and state taxes for those employees. The recent trials and tribulations of Zoe Baird and Kimba Wood[5] awakened the nation's awareness to the tax liabilities and responsibilities parents assume when they hire someone to care for their children. When you pay someone to care for your children, you may find yourself between a rock and a hard place. You face disobeying the law because your care provider wants to be paid in cash and not have her income reported to the IRS, or you choose to comply with the law and risk losing your care provider.

The black market network of child care workers is very strong, and states that do not have laws that require licensing of home care providers reinforce that network. These providers are less expensive than child day centers, and the proprietors demand payment in cash in order to

---

5. Both failed to win appointments to the position of U. S. Attorney General in the Clinton administration because they had not paid taxes for their child care workers.

avoid a paper trail that would alert the Internal Revenue Service to their additional income. They are working, earning, and not paying taxes on their income. They are also working for less than minimum wage scales. Parents who shop for the least expensive child care perpetuate this underground network. Parents end up paying less for child care when they use these providers, but they forfeit the child care deduction on their own tax returns because they cannot prove their child care costs.

More importantly, parents who use black market or underground sitters forfeit many of the benefits enjoyed by parents who use licensed centers. Most social service agencies can not follow up claims of abuse or neglect in child care placements if the care provider is not licensed, or at least registered with the state. The provider does not qualify for U.S.D.A. food funds to feed the little clients, and this means there are no safeguards for assuring that quality food is served to the children.

No one inspects the illegal sitter's premises to assure against lead poisoning from the painted walls and window sills, to detect tainted water, fire hazards, playground violations, or scalding water faucets. If these limitations concern you, there are two other options for you. You can increase your sitter's wages enough to cover the amount of the difference in pay that legal reporting procedures cost. Or, you can choose a provider who is licensed. Good child care is an investment in your child's future, and quality child care is expensive.

What does the tax law say exactly?

The law says that if you pay that provider over $50 during a three-month period (quarter), you have an FICA withholding, reporting, and contribution liability. This is the instructional paragraph taken directly from the instructions for Form 942, the *Employer's Quarterly Tax Return for Household Employees.*

Social Security and Medicare Taxes

Both the employer and the employee must pay social security and medicare taxes on cash wages the employee receives for household work in or around the employer's private home (not including a private home on a farm operated for profit). Generally, it includes services by cooks, waiters, waitresses, butlers, housekeepers, *governesses,* maids, cleaning people, valets, *baby-sitters,* janitors, laundresses, caretakers, handymen, gardeners, and drivers of cars for family use. The social security and medicare taxes are calculated separately because each tax has a different wage base. The combined social security tax rate is 12.4% (6.2% employer tax plus 6.2% employee tax). It applies to the first $57,600 of *cash* wages paid in a year. The combined medicare tax rate is 2.9% (1.45% employer tax plus 1.45% employee tax). This rate applies to the first $135,000 of cash wages paid in a year.

Congress is reworking this formula, and there will be changes if the recommendations of the Senate Finance Committee made on March 22, 1994 make it through the entire legislative process. That committee recommended employers be required to pay social security taxes on household employees who earn $630 in 1995. That amount would be collected first in 1996. Baby-sitters and yard workers under age 18 would be exempted.

Is the entire salary I pay my sitter subject to taxes?

If you paid more than $50 during a three-month period, you must pay taxes on all cash wages. Checks, money orders, etc., are the same as cash. If you provide food, lodging, clothing, bus tokens, or other non-cash items to your sitter, the value of those items is not subject to social security and medicare taxes. It does not matter whether you paid your employee by the hour, day, week, month, or year.

When and how do I pay these taxes?

First, you must obtain an EIN (employer identification number) from the Internal Revenue Service (Form SS-4). Then you must file Form 942 and pay quarterly. Form 942 is due the last day of March, June, September, and December. You can get these forms by calling the 800 number listed under the IRS (Internal Revenue Service) in your local telephone book. They will send you the necessary forms and instruction booklets. You should pay by check. If the new and simplified law passes, you will need to make annual payments only beginning in 1996.

Can I deduct the taxes from the sitter's wages?

You can deduct the appropriate amount from the sitter's wages, or you can pay the tax in addition to the wages. If you pay your sitter $4 an hour, you deduct 25 cents (6.2%) for social security and 6 cents (1.45%) for medicare, or 31 cents per hour. As the employer you must pay an equal amount as your contribution, so you send the IRS 62 cents for every hour your sitter works. The actual cost to you for that sitter is now $4.62 an hour. If you pay your sitter $40 a week, you would owe $6.20 to the IRS for each week.

Is Form 942 all I have to file?

Unfortunately, no. It is more complicated than just that one form. You must file Form 940 also, the Employer's Annual Federal Unemployment (FUTA) Tax Return. This form is filed yearly by January 31, and it requires a contribution of 6.2% of pay for unemployment insurance. That is an additional 25 cents per hour if you are paying your sitter $4 an hour. Your total cost for the sitter is now $4.87 an hour. There are similar state tax forms that are required in many states.

Is that the final form I file?

There is just one more piece of paperwork you must complete. You need to send a completed W-2 Wage and Tax Statement to the Social Security Administration and to your employee no later than January 31 of each year. According to the instructions for the W-2 form, "The time needed to complete and file this form will vary depending on individual circumstances. The estimated average time is 32 minutes." This form asks for the total wages you have paid, the total social security wages (total before taxes), and the amount of social security wages withheld. You will need to keep careful records of all payments to your employee and to the Internal Revenue Service. Of course, your sitter must file the income that you report on that W-2 form and they have to pay taxes on that amount.

As noted, there is ongoing discussion in Congress pointed toward making this complicated procedure easier and to changing the dollar limits currently set. It is obvious that the procedure is unwieldy, and you can understand why both Zoe Baird and Kimba Wood overlooked the required payments.

How does this reporting process affect my child care provider?

This signals a drastic change in her economic life. She can dwell no longer in the underground economy, and she has to begin paying taxes on what she earns, just as you pay taxes on your salary. It also establishes an earning record for her with the Social Security Administration, and that can affect her retirement earnings. It makes her eligible for unemployment benefits in the future.

*What are the penalties if you fail to file these
forms and pay these taxes and you get caught?*

A failure to pay the required withholding including employer contributions results in a 10% penalty. An additional penalty of up to 25% of the withholding including the employer's FICA contribution applies if the non-payment continues for six months. A penalty of up to 25% applies if there is also a failure to file the quarterly return. Finally, a 20% accuracy penalty applies to the failure to pay. Wilful failures to file quarterly reports and to make required payments can be criminally prosecuted (Davis, p. 7, VLW 1145).

Where can I get the correct IRS forms and more information?

Your telephone book lists an 800 number for the Internal Revenue Service. Call and request a copy of the IRS Publication 926, *Employment Taxes for Household Employers.* Copies of all these forms are in the appendix.

There are questions left unanswered for many of you, but, hopefully, some of the mystery of how preschools and child day centers operate is solved. You can go out and evaluate prospective placements, recognize their curricula choices, and judge where your child will be comfortable. Good luck!

REFERENCES

CHILD FIND STATEMENT, *The News and Daily Advance,* April 15, 1993, Lynchburg, Virginia.

Davis, C. Richard. (April 5, 1993) In the wake of Zoe Baird: Domestic employees. *Virginia Lawyers Weekly,* p. 7, VLW 1145.

Minimum Standards for Licensed Child Day Centers Serving Children of Preschool Age or Younger. July 8, 1993. Richmond, Virginia: Department of Social Services, Commonwealth of Virginia.

APPENDICES

Appendix A

CHILD DAY CARE CHECK SHEET

QUESTIONS TO ASK	YES	NO
Is this a licensed center?		
Do you have a copy of your policy manual that I could take home to study?		
Do you make arrangements to care for children when they become sick?		
Which meals do you serve? _____ Are they hot meals?		
Do I need to provide my own crib?		
Do you record diaper changes?		
Do you keep track of medications given?		
Can my child bring a favorite toy?		
Can I come eat lunch with my child occasionally?		
Do you take field trips with the children?		
Is your program developmentally appropriate?		
Do you have a van service for school-aged children?		

(Use the extra spaces for your own questions.)

Appendix B

OBSERVATIONS YOU MAKE

WHAT YOU OBSERVE—Outside	YES	NO
Is the playground spacious and well fenced?		
Are there soft landing spots under each piece of playground equipment?		
Are there blacktop areas for wheeled toys?		
Does the equipment appear well maintained?		
Is the sandbox covered at night?		
Are the pieces of playground equipment conducive to imaginative play?		
Inside		
Are there a number of center activities such as housekeeping, block corner, water table, painting/art, workshop, and a reading corner with a lot of books?		
Does the center have a bright, airy, CLEAN appearance?		
Are the children involved in happy play?		
Are the children's belongings kept in specially marked cubbies?		
Are drinking glasses marked with the children's names?		
Are the electrical sockets covered?		

(Use the extra spaces for your own questions.)

Appendix C
TAX FORMS

FORM 942

| Form **942** (Rev. July 1993) Department of the Treasury Internal Revenue Service | 4141 | **Employer's Quarterly Tax Return for Household Employees** (For Social Security, Medicare, and Withheld Income Taxes) See separate instructions. | OMB No. 1545-0034 |

Your name, address, employer identification number, and calendar quarter of return. (If not correct, please change.) ▶

Name

Address and ZIP code

Date quarter ended

Employer identification number
☐ – ☐

FOR IRS USE ONLY

If address is different from prior return, check here. ▶ ☐

Social security and Medicare taxes are due for each household employee to whom you paid cash wages of $50 or more in the calendar quarter covered by this return. For information on Federal Unemployment (FUTA) Tax, see page 1 of Instructions.

If you will **NOT** need to file Form 942 in the future, check here . . . . ▶ ☐

1 Total cash wages subject to social security taxes (see page 2 of Instructions) . | 1 |

2 Social security taxes (multiply line 1 by 12.4% (.124)) . . . . | 2 |
3 Total cash wages subject to Medicare taxes (see page 2 of Instructions) . | 3 |

4 Medicare taxes (multiply line 3 by 2.9% (.029)) . . . . | 4 |

5 Federal income tax withheld (if requested by your employee) (see page 2 of Instructions) . . . | 5 |

6 Total taxes (add lines 2, 4, and 5) . . . . | 6 |

7 Advance earned income credit (EIC) payments **ONLY**, if any (see page 1 of Instructions) . . . . | 7 |

8 Total taxes due (subtract line 7 from line 6). Pay this amount to the Internal Revenue Service. If no tax is due, write NONE . . . . | 8 |

Send Form 942 and your payment to your **Internal Revenue Service Center** (see **Where To File** on page 2 of Instructions).

Important: You **MUST** give a Form W-2 to each employee and file Copy A with the **Social Security Administration**—see page 3 of Instructions.

Under the penalties of perjury, I declare that I have examined this return, and to the best of my knowledge and belief, it is true, correct, and complete.

Signature of employer ▶   Date ▶

Cat. No. 10250E   Form **942** (Rev. 7-93)

See separate instructions for information on completing this form.

FORM SS-4

Form SS-4
(Rev. April 1991)
Department of the Treasury
Internal Revenue Service

Application for Employer Identification Number

(For use by employers and others. Please read the attached instructions before completing this form.)

EIN
OMB No. 1545-0003
Expires 4-30-94

Please type or print clearly.

1 Name of applicant (True legal name) (See instructions.)

2 Trade name of business, if different from name in line 1

3 Executor, trustee, "care of" name

4a Mailing address (street address) (room, apt., or suite no.)

5a Address of business (See instructions.)

4b City, state, and ZIP code

5b City, state, and ZIP code

6 County and state where principal business is located

7 Name of principal officer, grantor, or general partner (See instructions.) ▶

8a Type of entity (Check only one box.) (See instructions.)
- ☐ Individual SSN _____
- ☐ REMIC
- ☐ State/local government
- ☐ Other nonprofit organization (specify) _____
- ☐ Other (specify) ▶ _____
- ☐ Estate
- ☐ Plan administrator SSN _____
- ☐ Personal service corp.
- ☐ National guard
- ☐ Other corporation (specify) _____
- ☐ Federal government/military
- ☐ Trust
- ☐ Partnership
- ☐ Farmers' cooperative
- ☐ Church or church controlled organization

If nonprofit organization enter GEN (if applicable) _____

8b If a corporation, give name of foreign country (if applicable) or state in the U.S. where incorporated ▶

Foreign country | State

9 Reason for applying (Check only one box.)
- ☐ Started new business
- ☐ Hired employees
- ☐ Created a pension plan (specify type) ▶ _____
- ☐ Banking purpose (specify) ▶ _____
- ☐ Changed type of organization (specify) ▶ _____
- ☐ Purchased going business
- ☐ Created a trust (specify) ▶ _____
- ☐ Other (specify) ▶ _____

10 Date business started or acquired (Mo., day, year) (See instructions.)

11 Enter closing month of accounting year. (See instructions.)

12 First date wages or annuities were paid or will be paid (Mo., day, year). **Note:** *If applicant is a withholding agent, enter date income will first be paid to nonresident alien. (Mo., day, year)* . . . . ▶

13 Enter highest number of employees expected in the next 12 months. **Note:** *If the applicant does not expect to have any employees during the period, enter "0."* . . . . . . ▶

Nonagricultural	Agricultural	Household

14 Principal activity (See instructions.) ▶

15 Is the principal business activity manufacturing? . . . . ☐ Yes ☐ No
If "Yes," principal product and raw material used ▶

16 To whom are most of the products or services sold? Please check the appropriate box. ☐ Business (wholesale)
☐ Public (retail) ☐ Other (specify) ▶   ☐ N/A

17a Has the applicant ever applied for an identification number for this or any other business? . . . . ☐ Yes ☐ No
Note: *If "Yes," please complete lines 17b and 17c.*

17b If you checked the "Yes" box in line 17a, give applicant's true name and trade name, if different than name shown on prior application.

True name ▶ | Trade name ▶

17c Enter approximate date, city, and state where the application was filed and the previous employer identification number if known.
Approximate date when filed (Mo., day, year) | City and state where filed | Previous EIN

Under penalties of perjury, I declare that I have examined this application, and to the best of my knowledge and belief, it is true, correct, and complete. | Telephone number (include area code)

Name and title (Please type or print clearly.) ▶

Signature ▶ | Date ▶

Note: *Do not write below this line.   For official use only.*

Please leave blank ▶	Geo.	Ind.	Class	Size	Reason for applying

For Paperwork Reduction Act Notice, see attached instructions.   Cat. No. 16055N   Form **SS-4** (Rev. 4-91)

FORM 940

Form 940
Department of the Treasury
Internal Revenue Service

Employer's Annual Federal Unemployment (FUTA) Tax Return

▶ For Paperwork Reduction Act Notice, see separate instructions.

OMB No. 1545-0028

1992

T	
FF	
FD	
FP	
I	
T	

If incorrect, make any necessary change. ▶

Name (as distinguished from trade name)   Calendar year

Trade name, if any

Address and ZIP code   Employer identification number

	Yes	No
A	Are you required to pay unemployment contributions to only one state?	☐	☐
B	Did you pay all state unemployment contributions by February 1, 1993? (If a 0% experience rate is granted check "Yes.")	☐	☐
C	Were all wages that were taxable for FUTA tax also taxable for your state's unemployment tax?	☐	☐
D	Did you pay all wages in a state other than Michigan?	☐	☐

If you answered "No" to any of these questions, you must file Form 940. If you answered "Yes" to all the questions, you may file Form 940-EZ which is a simplified version of Form 940. You can get Form 940-EZ by calling 1-800-TAX-FORM (1-800-829-3676).

If you will not have to file returns in the future, check here, complete, and sign the return . . . . ▶ ☐
If this is an Amended Return, check here . . . . ▶ ☐

Part I   **Computation of Taxable Wages**

		Amount paid		
1	Total payments (including exempt payments) during the calendar year for services of employees.		1	
2	Exempt payments. (Explain each exemption shown, attach additional sheets if necessary.) ▶	2		
3	Payments of more than $7,000 for services. Enter only amounts over the first $7,000 paid to each employee. Do not include payments from line 2. The $7,000 amount is the Federal wage base. Your state wage base may be different. **Do not use the state wage limitation**	3		
4	Total exempt payments (add lines 2 and 3)		4	
5	**Total taxable wages** (subtract line 4 from line 1) . . . . ▶		5	
6	Additional tax resulting from credit reduction for unrepaid advances to the State of Michigan. Enter the wages included on line 5 for Michigan and multiply by .011. (See the separate Instructions for Form 940.) Enter the credit reduction amount here and in Part II, line 5: Michigan wages _____ × .011 = ... ▶		6	

Be sure to complete both sides of this return and sign in the space provided on the back.   Cat. No. 11234O   Form **940** (1992)

FORM 940 continued

Form 940 (1992)   Page **2**

Part II   **Tax Due or Refund**

1. Gross FUTA tax. Multiply the wages in Part I, line 5, by .062 . . . . **1**
2. Maximum credit. Multiply the wages in Part I, line 5, by .054 . . . | **2** |
3. **Computation of tentative credit:**

(a) Name of state	(b) State reporting number(s) as shown on employer's state contribution returns	(c) Taxable payroll (as defined in state act)	(d) State experience rate		(e) State experience rate	(f) Contributions if rate had been 5.4% (col. (c) x .054)	(g) Contributions payable at experience rate (col. (c) x col. (e))	(h) Additional credit (col. (f) minus col.(g)). If 0 or less, enter 0.	(i) Contributions actually paid to state
			From	To					

3a. Totals ▶

3b. **Total tentative credit** (add line 3a, columns (h) and (i) only—see instructions for limitations on late payments) ▶

4. **Credit:** Enter the smaller of the amount in Part II, line 2, or line 3b . | **4** |
5. Enter the amount from Part I, line 6 . . . . **5**
6. **Credit allowable** (subtract line 5 from line 4). (If zero or less, enter 0.) **6**
7. **Total FUTA tax** (subtract line 6 from line 1) **7**
8. Total FUTA tax deposited for the year, including any overpayment applied from a prior year . . **8**
9. **Balance due** (subtract line 8 from line 7). This should be $100 or less. Pay to the Internal Revenue Service . . . . ▶ **9**
10. **Overpayment** (subtract line 7 from line 8). Check if it is to be: ☐ **Applied to next return,** or ☐ **Refunded** . . . . ▶ **10**

Part III   **Record of Quarterly Federal Tax Liability for Unemployment Tax** *(Do not include state liability)*

Quarter	First	Second	Third	Fourth	Total for year
Liability for quarter					

Under penalties of perjury, I declare that I have examined this return, including accompanying schedules and statements, and to the best of my knowledge and belief, it is true, correct, and complete, and that no part of any payment made to a state unemployment fund claimed as a credit was or is to be deducted from the payments to employees.

Signature ▶   Title (Owner, etc.) ▶   Date ▶

FORM W-2

a Control number		Void ☐			
b Employer's identification number			1 Wages, tips, other compensation	2 Federal income tax withheld
c Employer's name, address, and ZIP code			3 Social security wages	4 Social security tax withheld
			5 Medicare wages and tips	6 Medicare tax withheld
			7 Social security tips	8 Allocated tips
d Employee's social security number			9 Advance EIC payment	10 Dependent care benefits
e Employee's name, address, and ZIP code			11 Nonqualified plans	12 Benefits included in Box 1
			13	14 Other
			15 Statutory employee ☐ Deceased ☐ Pension plan ☐ Legal rep. ☐ 942 emp ☐ Subtotal ☐ Deferred compensation ☐	
16 State	Employer's state I.D. No.	17 State wages, tips, etc.	18 State income tax	19 Locality name	20 Local wages, tips, etc.	21 Local income tax

Department of the Treasury—Internal Revenue Service

Form W-2 Wage and Tax Statement **1993**

Copy 1 For State, City, or Local Tax Department

OMB No. 1545-0008

Appendix D

LICENSING AND RESOURCE & REFERRAL SERVICES BY STATE LISTING

ALABAMA
Office of Day Care and Child
  Development
Dept. of Human Resources
64 N. Union Street
Montgomery, AL 36130
Call (205) 261-3409

Alabama Association for CCR&R
  Agencies
309 N. 23rd Street
Birmingham, AL 35203
Call (205) 252-1991

ALASKA
Community Care Coordinator
Division of Family and Youth Services
Dept. of Health and Social Services
Box H-05
Juneau, AK 99811
Call (907) 465-2145

Alaska CCR&R Alliance
Box 103394
Anchorage, AK 99510
Call (907) 279-5024

ARIZONA
Office of Child Day Care Facilities
Dept. of Health Services
411 N. 24th Street
Phoenix, AZ 85008
Call (602) 255-1272

Tucson Assc. for Child Care
1030 N. Alvernon Way
Tucson, AZ 85711
Call (602) 881-8940

ARKANSAS
Dept. of Human Services
Div. of Children and Family
626 Donaghey Bldg.
7th and Main Streets
Box 1437
Little Rock, AR 72203
Call (501) 371-2651

Arkansas Child Care Resource Center
5 Statehouse Plaza
Little Rock, AR 72201
Call (501) 375-3690

CALIFORNIA
Children's Day Care/Administrative
  Support Bureau
Dept. of Social Services
744 P Street, Mail Station 19-50
Sacramento, CA 95814
Call (916) 324-4031

California CCR&R Network
111 New Montgomery, 7th Floor
San Francisco, CA 94105
Call (415) 882-0234

COLORADO
Child Welfare Division
Dept. of Social Services
1575 Sherman St.
Denver, CO 80203
Call (303) 866-5942

Colorado Office of R&R Agencies
7853 E. Arapahoe Rd., Suite 3300
Englewood, CO 80112
Call (303) 290-9088

CONNECTICUT

United Way of Conn/Infoline
900 Asylum Ave.
Hartford, CT 06105
Call (203) 249-6850

Center and Group Home Care:
  Day Care Licensing
Dept. of Health Services
150 Washington St.
Hartford, CT 06115
Call (203) 566-3737

DELAWARE

Child Care Connection
3411 Silverside Rd., Baynard #100
Wilmington, DE 19810
Call (302) 479-1660

Licensing Services
Division of Child Protection
Dept. of Services for Child, Youth and
  Families
330 E. 30th St., 3rd Floor
Wilmington, DE 19802
Call (302) 571-6410

DISTRICT OF COLUMBIA

Washington Child Development Council
2121 Decatur Place, NW
Washington, DC 20008
Call (202) 387-0002

Day Care Licensing
Dept. of Consumer & Regulatory Affairs
614 H Street, NW, Rm. 1031
Washington, DC 20001
Call (202) 727-7226

FLORIDA

Florida Children's Forum
1282 Paul Russell Rd.
Tallahassee, FL 32301
Call (904) 656-2272

Child Care & Prevention Unit
Dept. of Health and Rehab. Services
1317 Winewood Blvd., Bldg. 6 Rm. 450
Tallahassee, FL 32399
Call (904) 488-4900

GEORGIA

Child Care Solutions
1340 Spring St. NW, Suite 200
Atlanta, GA 30306
Call (404) 885-1578

Day Care Licensing Section
Office of Regulatory Services
Dept. of Human Resources
878 Peach St., NE, Rm. 808
Atlanta, GA 30309
Call (404) 894-5688

HAWAII

Patch
810 A Vineyard Blvd.
Honolulu, HI 96734
Call (808) 842-3874

Prog. Admin. Day Care
Dept. of Social Services
Box 339
Honolulu, HI 96809
Call (808) 548-2302

IDAHO

Child Care Connections
Box 6756
Boise, ID 83707
Call (208) 343-5437

Day Care Licensing
Bureau of Social Services
Idaho Dept. of Health & Welfare
State House
Boise, ID 83720
Call (208) 334-5702

ILLINOIS

Illinois CCR&R System
100 W. Randolph, Suite 6-206
Chicago, IL 60601
Call (312) 814-5524

Dept. of Children & Family Serv.
406 E. Monroe
Springfield, IL 62701
Call (217) 785-2598

INDIANA
Indiana Assc. for CCR&R
4460 Guion Rd.
Indianapolis, IN 46254
Call (317) 299-2750

Day Care Services
Child Welfare & Soc. Services
141 S. Meridian, 6th Floor
Indianapolis, IN 46225
Call (317) 232-4521

IOWA
Polk Co. Child Care & Resource
1200 University, Suite F
Des Moines, IA 50314
Call (515) 286-2004

Bureau of Adult, Children & Family
  Services
Dept. of Human Services
5th Floor, Hoover State Office Bldg.
Des Moines, IA 50319
Call (515) 281-6074

KANSAS
Child Care Assc. of Wichita
1069 Parklane Office Park
Wichita, KS 67218
Call (316) 682-1853

Bureau of Adult and Child Care
Dept. of Health and Environment
900 S.W. Jackson
Topeka, KS 66620
Call (913) 296-1272

KENTUCKY
Child Care Council of KY
880 Sparta Ct., #100
Lexington, KY 40504
Call (606) 254-9176

Cabinet for Human Resources
Fourth Floor East
275 E. Main St.
Frankfort, KY 40621
Call (502) 564-2800

LOUISIANA
Child Care Information, Inc.
Box 45212, D 223
Baton Rouge, LA 70895
Call (504) 293-8523

Div. of Licensing and Certification
Dept. of Health and Human Services
Box 3767
Baton Rouge, LA 70821
Call (504) 342-5774

MAINE
Maine Assc. of CCR&R Agencies
Box 280 WHCA
Milbridge, ME 04658
Call (207) 546-7544

Licensing Unit
Dept. of Human Services
State House Station 11
Augusta, ME 04333
Call (207) 289-5060

MARYLAND
Maryland Child Care Resource Network
608 Water St.
Baltimore, MD 21202
Call (301) 752-7588

Dept. of Human Resources
Office of Child Care and Regulation
311 W. Saratoga St.
Baltimore, MD 21202
Call (301) 333-1985

MASSACHUSETTS
Exec. Office for Health & Hum. Ser.
1 Ashburton Pl., 11th Floor
Boston, MA 02108
Call (617) 727-8900

Office for Children
150 Causeway St.
Boston, MA 02133
Call (617) 727-8900

MICHIGAN
Michigan 4C Assc.
2875 Northwind Dr., #200

East Lansing, MI 48823
Call (517) 351-4171

Day Care Licensing
Dept. of Social Services
300 S. Capital, Box 30037
Lansing, MI 48909
Call (517) 373-8300

MINNESOTA
Minnesota CCR&R Network
2116 Campus Dr. SE
Rochester, MN 55904
Call (507) 287-2497

Dept. of Human Services
Space Center, 6th Floor
444 Lafayette Rd.
St. Paul, MN 55101
Call (612) 296-3768

MISSISSIPPI
Office for Children & Youth
421 W. Pascagoula St.
Jackson, MS 39203
Call (601) 949-2054

Child Care Licensure Div.
Bureau of Personal Health
St. Dept. of Health, Box 1700
Jackson, MS 39205
Call (601) 960-7740

MISSOURI
Heart of America Family Services
3217 Broadway #500
Kansas City, MO 64111
Call (816) 753-5280

State Day Care Supervisor
Div. of Family Services
Broadway St. Office Bldg., Box 88
Jefferson City, MO 65103
Call (314) 751-2450

MONTANA
Early Childhood Project
Montana State University
Bozeman, MT 59717
Call (406) 994-5005

Community Services Division
Dept. of Social and Rehab. Services
Box 4210
Helena, MT 59604
Call (406) 444-3865

NEBRASKA
Midwest Child Care Assc.
5015 Dodge #2
Omaha, NE 68132
Call (402) 551-2379

Day Care Licensing Consultant
Dept. of Social Services
Box 95026
Lincoln, NE 68509
Call (402) 471-3121

NEVADA
Child Care Resource Council
1090 S. Rock Boulevard
Reno, NV 89502
Call (702) 785-4200

Bureau of Services for Child Care
Dept. of Human Resources
Rm. 606, Kinkead Bldg.
505 E. King St.
Carson City, NV 89710
Call (702) 885-5911

NEW HAMPSHIRE
New Hampshire Assc. of CCR&R
  Agencies
99 Hanover St., Box 448
Manchester, NH 03105
Call (603) 668-1920

Child Care Standards and Licensing
Div. of Health and Welfare
6 Hazen Dr.
Concord, NH 00301
Call (603) 271-4624

NEW JERSEY
Statewide Clearinghouse/Div. of Y & F
  Services
Capitol Center
50 E. State St., CN 717

Trenton, NJ 08625
Call (609) 292-8408

Bureau of Licensing
Div. of Youth and Family Services
Dept. of Human Services
1 S. Montgomery St.
Trenton, NJ 08625
Call (609) 292-1018

NEW MEXICO
Las Cruces CCR&R
Box 30001, Dept. 3CUR
Las Cruces, NM 88003
Call (505) 646-1165

Public Health Division
Box 968
Santa Fe, NM 87504
Call (505) 827-2448

NEW YORK
New York State Child Care
  Coordinating Council
237 Bradford St.
Albany, NY 12206
Call (518) 463-8663

Dept. of Social Services, Day Care
  Licensing Unit
330 Broadway
Albany, NY 12243
Call (518) 432-2763

NORTH CAROLINA
North Carolina CCR&R Network
700 Kenilworth Ave.
Charlotte, NC 28204
Call (704) 376-6697

Child Day Care Section
Div. of Facility Services
Dept. of Human Resources
701 Barbour Dr.
Raleigh, NC 27603
Call (919) 733-4801

NORTH DAKOTA
North Dakota Early Childhood
  Training Center
Box 5057, ND State University
Fargo, ND 58105
Call (701) 237-8289

Dept. of Human Services
Office of Children and Family
State Capitol Bldg.
Bismarck, ND 58505
Call (701) 224-2316

OHIO
Ohio CCR&R Assc.
92 Jefferson Ave.
Columbus, OH 43215
Call (614) 224-0222

Child Care Regulation Unit
Bureau of Child Care Services
30 E. Broad St.
Columbus, OH 43266
Call (614) 466-3822

OKLAHOMA
Child Care Resource Center
1430 South Boulder
Tulsa, OK 74119
Call (918) 585-5551

Day Care Licensing Service Unit
Dept. of Human Services
Box 25352
Oklahoma City, OK 73125
Call (405) 521-3561

OREGON
CCR&R of Linn & Benton Counties
6500 SW Pacific Blvd.
Albany, OR 97321
Call (503) 967-6501

Day Care Unit
Children's Services Division
Dept. of Human Resources
198 Commercial St. SE
Salem, OR 97310
Call (503) 378-3178

PENNSYLVANIA
Child Care Choices Resource & Referral
1233 Locust Street, 3rd Floor

Philadelphia, PA 19107
Call (215) 985-3355

Bureau of Child Dev. Programs
Office of Policy, Planning & Eval.
Dept. of Public Welfare
Box 2675
Harrisburg, PA 17105
Call (800) 222-2117

RHODE ISLAND
Options for Working Parents
30 Exchange Terrace
Commerce Center
Providence, RI 02903
Call (401) 272-7510

Dept. for Children & Their Families
Day Care Licensing Unit
610 Mt. Pleasant St.
Providence, RI 02908
Call (401) 457-4540

SOUTH CAROLINA
South Carolina CCR&R Network/Co Yes, Inc.
2129 Santee Ave.
Columbia, SC 29205
Call (803) 254-9263

Licensing Div. Children,
Family and Adult Services
Box 1520
Columbia, SC 29202
Call (803) 734-5740

SOUTH DAKOTA
SDSU/DHD Child & Family Studies
Box 2218
Brookings, SD 57007
Call (605) 688-5730

Child Protection
Dept. of Social Services
Kneip Bldg.
700 N. Illinois St.
Pierre, SD 57501
Call (605) 773-3227

TENNESSEE
Tennessee CRR&R Services
Tennessee DHS/Day Care Services
Nashville, TN 37248
Call (615) 741-3312

Day Care Licensing Division
Dept. of Human Services
400 Deaderick St.
Nashville, TN 37219
Call (615) 741-7129

TEXAS
TACCRRA, c/o Austin Families
3307 Northland Dr., #460
Austin, TX 78731
Call (512) 440-8555

Day Care Licensing
Dept. of Human Resources
Box 15995
Austin, TX 78761
Call (512) 835-2350

UTAH
Office of Child Care
324 S. State St., #500
Salt Lake City, UT 84111
Call (801) 538-8695

Office of Licensing
Dept. of Social Services
120 N. 200th, West
Salt Lake City, UT 84103
Call (801) 538-4242

VERMONT
VACCRRA
Early Childhood Prgms.
Vermont College
Montpelier, VT 05602
Call (802) 828-8771

Children's Day Care Unit
Dept. of Social and Rehab. Services
103 S. Main St.
Waterbury, VT 05676
Call (802) 241-2158

VIRGINIA
Virginia Child Care Resource & Referral Network
3701 Pender Dr.
Fairfax, VA 22030
Call (703) 218-3730

Div. of Licensing Programs
Dept. of Social Services
8007 Discovery Dr.
Richmond, VA 23229
Call (804) 662-9032

WASHINGTON
Washington State CCR&R Network
917 Pacific Ave., #301
Tacoma, WA 98402
Call (206) 383-1735

Div. of Children and Family Services
Dept. of Social and Health Services
Olympia, WA 98504
Call (206) 753-7002

WEST VIRGINIA
Central Child Care of WV, Inc.
Box 5340
Charleston, WV 25361
Call (304) 340-3667

Day Care Licensing Unit
West Virginia Dept. of Human Services
Capitol Complex
Bldg. 6, Room 850
Charleston, WV 25305
Call (304) 348-7980

WISCONSIN
WICC Improvement Project
202 S. Dakota Ave., Box 369
Hayward, WI 54843
Call (715) 643-3905

Bureau for Children, Youth and Families
Dept. of Health and Social Services
Box 7851
Madison, WI 53707
Call (608) 266-8200

WYOMING
Care Connections, Inc
125 College Dr.
CC Family Res. Ctr.
Casper, WY 82601
Call (307) 472-5535

Family Services Unit
Dept. of Health and Social Services
Hathaway Bldg.
Cheyenne, WY 82002
Call (307) 777-5994

INDEX

A

Associative play, definition, 10
"Au pair" child care givers, 52
Autism
  characteristics of, 71
  definition, 71

B

Blindness, definition, 73–74
Bragdon, Nancy H., 24, 45, 57, 68
Bredekamp, S., 7, 13
Brown, C. C., 13

C

Caldwell, B. M., 10, 13
Child day care
  checklist, illustration, 83, 84
  for ages eighteen months to three years, 25–34
    accomplishments during, 25
    care in unlicensed baby sitter's home, 30–31
    child care options for, 27–33
    guidelines for search of, 34
    licensed family day-care homes, 31
    part-time options for, 33–34
    playing outside, 27
    playing with others, 25–26
    safe environment for, 26
    use appropriate learning activities, 27
  for children with special needs, 69–74
    education for, 69–70
    locating resources, 70–71
    recognition handicapping disabilities, 71–74
  for five year olds, 58–68
    beginning school (*see* Kindergarten)
    care of by a relative, 62–63
    full-day child care options for, 62–67
    guidelines for locating child care, 67–68
    sitter in your home, 63–64
  for four-year olds, 46–57
    age of playmates, 48–49
    by child day centers, 55
    characteristics of four year olds, 46
    full-day options for, 51–56
    guidelines for child care search, 56–57
    half versus full-day preschool programs, 49–50
    half-day options for, 50–51
    incidence classroom attendance by, 46
    need for developmentally appropriate activities, 49
    reading to, 47
    use of five-day preschool program, 47
  for three-year-olds, 35–45
    benefits of half-day programs, 38–39
    biting by child, 37
    full-day child care options for, 39–44
    guidelines for child day care, 44–45
    half-day programs for, 36
    learning to play with other children, 36–37
    use of television by sitter, 37
  for infants (*see* Infant child care)
  for parents working unusual hours, 74–76
    employer-sponsored centers, 75–76
    shift sharing, 75
    teenage sitters, 75
  legal and tax responsibilities for, 76–80 (*see also* Legal & tax responsibilities)
Children's play (*see* Play)

Church programs for four to five year olds, 50–51, 61–62
Cooperative play, definition, 10

D

Davis, C. Richard, 80
Day-care homes
  licensed, 21–22
  unlicensed sitter, 20–21
Deaf-blindness, definition, 72
Deafness, definition, 72
Developmentally appropriate practices for children, 7–13
  guidelines for, 6–7
  play centers for, 10–12
  whole group activities, 7–8
  writing alphabet letters, 7
DeVries, R., 13
Dramatic play centers, use of, 10–11

E

Early childhood education
  behaviorist approach to, 4–5
  constructivist approach to, 4, 5–6
  curriculum approaches to, 6–13
    developmentally appropriate practices, 6–8
    emerging literacy guidelines, 8–9
    play, 9–13 (*see also* Play)
  romanticist approach to, 4, 5
Elkind, David, 24, 45, 57, 60, 68
Emerging literacy, 8–9
Employer Identification Number (SS-4), 78, 87
Employer-sponsored child day centers
  at child day centers, 22
  at place of business, 23
  for children aged 18 to 36 months, 32–33
  for five year olds, 56
  for four year olds, 56
  for parents working unusual hours, 75–76
  for three year olds, 44
Employer's Annual Federal Unemployment Tax Return (Form 940), 88–89
Employer's Quarterly Tax Return for Household Employees (Form 942), 86

F

Form 9420
  illustration, 88–89
  use of, 79
Form 942
  illustration, 86
  use of, 78, 79
Form SS-4
  illustration, 87
  use of, 78
Froebel, Friedrich, 4
Frost, J. L., 13

G

Gottfried, A. W., 13

H

Head Start, 50
Hearing impairment, definition, 72
Henry, Tamara, 13

I

Illiteracy, rate of in adults, 9
Infant child care (birth to eighteen months), 14–24
  checklists, 83, 84
  child day centers, 22–23
  cuddling and security for, 14
  employer-sponsored, 23–24
  healthy and safe environment for, 14–15
  in baby-sitter's home, 20–21
  leaving crying child with sitter, 16
  licensed family day-care home, 21
  major needs of baby, 14–15
  mother's care following child day care, 23
  options available for, 17–20
  promotion language development, 14, 15
  special notes for, 24

K

Katzev, Aphra R., 24, 45, 57, 68

Index

Kindergarten
    academic activities in, 9
    alternative church and private school
        programs, 61–62
    alternatives for beginning, 61
    factors in age to begin, 58–59
    origin of term, 4
    preentrance test for, 60
    writing experience prior to, 60–61
Kohlberg, L., 13

L

Language development of child
    birth to eighteen months, 15–16
    impairment of, definition, 73
    of three year olds, 35
    regulations for, 16–17
Language impairment, definition, 73
Legal & tax responsibilities for child care,
    76–80
    advantages of, 77
    deductions from wages, 78–79, 80
    failure to pay, 76–77
    IRS forms used, 78–79
        illustrations, 86, 87, 88–89, 90
        obtaining forms, 80
    Medicare tax, 77–78
    payment of taxes, 78–80
    sitter's income as taxable, 79, 80
    social security taxes, 77
    tax law, 77
    wages taxable, 78
Licensed family day-care homes
    for 18 to 36 month olds, 31
    for 3 year olds, 42–43
    for 4 year olds, 54–55
    for 5 year olds, 65–66
Licensing and resource and referral services
    by state, 91–97
Lusk, Diane, 24, 45, 57, 68

M

McPherson, Bruce, 24, 45, 57, 68
Medicare tax, on child care wages,
    77–78
Mental retardation, definition, 72
Montessori, 9

Mother's Day Out Programs, 50
Multiple disabilities, definition, 72

N

Nannie care
    for children 18 to 36 months old, 28–30
    for five year olds, 63
    for three year olds, 39, 40
    for four year olds, 52
    use of, 18–19
    wages for, 19

O

Onlooker children, definition, 10
Orthopedic impairment, definition, 72

P

Parallel activity, definition, 10
Parten, M. B., 10, 13
Play in preschool/child day centers
    art/writing center, 11–12
    as child's work, 9–10
    associative play, 10
    block center, 11
    book centers, 12
    cooperative play, 10
    developmentally appropriate, 10–11
    dramatic play centers, 10–11
    indoor/outdoor equipment for, 12
    music centers, 12
    onlooker children, definition, 10
    parallel activity, 10
    relationship academic failure to lack of
        early, 9
    role of, 9–10
    science centers, 12
    sensory center, 12
    solitary independent player, 10
    symbolic, 10
    types of, 10
    unoccupied children defined, 10
    woodworking center, 12
Preschool/child day centers
    personal toys at, 17
    regulations for infant child day centers,
        16–17

Private School programs for four–five year olds, 50–51, 61–62
Public School Programs for four year olds, 50

R

Reading
    readiness for, 8, 47–48
    to children, 9, 35
Rogers, C. S., 10, 13

S

Sawyers, J. K., 10, 13
Serious emotional disturbance, definition, 72–73
Shepard, L. S., 9, 13
Smith, M. L., 9, 13
Social Security tax on child care wages, 77–78
Solitary independent player, definition, 10
Special needs children (see Child care for children with special needs)
Specific learning disability, definition, 73
Speech impairment, definition, 73

U

Unlicensed baby-sitter, 30–31
    for 18 to 36 month olds, 30–31
    for five year olds, 64–65
    for four year olds, 53–54
    for three year olds, 41
Unoccupied children, definition, 10

W

W-2 Wages and Tax statement
    illustration, 90
    use of, 79
Wages and Tax Statement (W-2), 90